`The Old Familiar Faces` -

Poems on the Experience of Ageing

ed.

Sybil Oldfield and Gwenyth Shaw

`I have had playmates, I have had companions, ...
All, all are gone, the old familiar faces.`

(Charles Lamb)

2007

This paperback ed. published in 2007 by Oldfield and Shaw.

British Library Cataloguing-in-Publication Data
A catalogue record for this book is available from the British Library

ISBN 978-0-9554114-1-0

Cover design by Keith Hunt, University of Sussex Print and Reprographic Unit

Printed and bound in Great Britain

Book orders £5.00 plus £2.00 p&p from:
Sybil Oldfield, 4 Houndean Close, Lewes, East Sussex, BN7 1EZ
Email: sib@larksrest.freeserve.co.uk

[Question]:

What shall I do with this absurdity –
O heart, O troubled heart – this caricature,
Decrepit age that has been tied to me
As to a dog's tail ?...

(Yeats, The Tower)

[Answer]:

An aged man is but a paltry thing,
A tattered coat upon a stick unless
Soul clap its hands and sing, and louder sing
For every tatter in its mortal dress…

(Yeats, Sailing to Byzantium)

CONTENTS

Introduction

`... emotions do not grow old.`

Why the title – The Old Familiar Faces? We thought it could evoke loved poems as well as the irreplaceable people who have accompanied us through life. And the sub-title? We wanted poems written from *inside* the experience of ageing.

In addition, each themed section of the book begins with a `Motto` page of short, often familiar passages, not necessarily written by the pensioned-off, but all speaking to our condition. For older people do not read only older people – we have been sustained over our lives by many a quotation from younger strengths. And we also included one section, `Being Loved`, which is not written by older people at all but by the young or middle-aged in response to their own special old ones.

But must not an anthology on `Ageing` be dully depressing if it is to be at all honest? The decay of every faculty in turn, deprivation of meaningful occupation, the loss of `precious friends hid in death's dateless night`, long painful illness and bodily indignities while the inevitable terminus awaits. Not a lot of laughs there. But a moment's reflection reminds us that `ageing`, for grown-ups, is just another word for `living`. We do not want to sound like grey-haired Pollyannas, but loving and laughing can continue to be facts of life, with any luck, to the end.

Readers will find in these pages, therefore, poems of late-flowering romantic love side by side with loves which have retained their fire over many years, as well as poems celebrating the many other forms that love may take. And there is no shortage of laughter, found not only in the section `Seeing the funny side` but also in other sections where humour will keep breaking out: take, for instance, the wry but loving humour of UA Fanthorpe's tribute to her mother in `Fanfare` or the self-mocking humour of Robert Graves in `The Face in the Mirror` when, after an unforgiving delineation of his own decaying features, he asks himself `why / He still stands ready, with a boy's presumption, / To court the queen in her high silk pavilion.`

Our anthology may strike readers as not having much to say about the relief and contentment experienced when one's children have left home, when one has retired from work with free time at last - and a pension permits modest self-indulgence. But `The pension pennies [do] trickle from the bank` in Lotte Kramer's `Stocktaking`, while Elaine Feinstein has managed to capture, in `Getting Older`, many reasons for happiness as she begins:

`The first surprise: I like it.`

One unusual feature of this anthology is that every section, except 'Having faith', begins with translations from Chinese poetry. We were amazed by how often those ancient writers had been before us in experience, and yet they sounded so contemporary. It made us feel that the whole world was indeed one very old town of continuous habitation. We were anxious that most of our chosen poems, although convincingly personal, should not be exclusively introspective but rather embrace engagement with others and with the world outside. For do we not all lead three lives – the secret life inside our heads, the life of personal relationship and life as citizens of our place and time? And this, it seems, had been just as true for the Chinese over a thousand years ago.

For reasons of shyness or reserve, the secret life inside our heads and the life of personal relationship frequently overlap because we so often lack the courage to declare our feelings. The poet who can overcome inhibition and express very personal emotion – as Elizabeth Jennings does in her poem 'Friendship'- makes a generous gift to us, her readers. Perhaps even greater is the generosity of those poets who write of personal heartbreak so powerfully that we share a little of their pain. Is such shared pain depressing? Surely what we feel most on reading, say, Edna St. Vincent Millay's 'Time does not bring relief', is a sense of gratitude to her for reaching out to us all in her struggle to be emotionally honest with herself.

To return to our three lives – the secret life inside our heads also overlaps with our life as citizens of our place and time. John Clare's elegy `Remembrances` starts with his rapturous memories of

> … jumping time away on old crossberry way
> And eating awes like sugar plums ere they had lost the may
> And skipping like a leveret before the peep of day
> On the rolly poly up and down of pleasant Swordy Well

but ends in despair over his flattened landscape where `Inclosure like a Buonaparte let not a thing remain/It levelled every bush and tree and levelled every hill`. As we age, we all have to witness change, not all of it for the worse, of course, but much of it experienced as loss. As Philip Larkin says in `Reference Back`:

> We are not suited to the long perspectives
> Open at each instant of our lives.
> They link us to our losses: worse,
> They show us what we have as it once was,
> Blindingly undiminished, just as though
> By acting differently, we could have kept it so.

Later, in the section `Resisting`, come poems by three women, `Aunt` Molly Jackson, Mary Brooksbank and Muriel Rukeyser, who did try to persuade people into `acting differently` and so make life better. For it is too often forgotten that behind the mask of old age there may often lie inextinguishable memories of the Depression, World War and the Holocaust (see Lotte Kramer) – and of the effort to resist as well as to survive.

But perhaps the bravest section of the anthology is `Lying Awake at Night`, where you will find two of our greatest poets, Yeats and Eliot, being preyed upon by shame at memories of words and acts `done to others' harm`. Here too is Philip Larkin owning up to his obsessive fear of death, for which he could find no relief or antidote. It is not easy to admit to shame and fear, or for that matter, to foolish behaviour and `miniature betrayals` - as Fleur Adcock helps us all by doing, even managing rueful humour, in her confessional poem `Things`.

The anthology ends with the poetry of religious faith and the poetry of humanist acceptance. Whether one believes or not in immortality, who does not respond to the depth of yearning behind so much of the powerful, beautiful language of religion? Who could not be moved by the vision of the tears being wiped from all eyes, or by Henry King's touching conviction of reunion with his wife: `slow howe'er my approaches be/I shall at last lie down by thee`? But `Having faith` does not have the last word in this book; instead, our final section is `Sleeping at Last` where poets express their sense of peace, when we need `Fear no more the heat o' the sun` and Death is `end and remedy`.

Of course we, the editors, did not always agree as we compiled this anthology. One of us wanted to be stricter than the other about the minimum qualifying age for a poet claiming to write about the experience of ageing. Was it really enough that he or she should *feel* old, or know that they were approaching death? One of us was tempted to be over-protective of the reader and cut the most painful poems; she needed to be reminded that our readers would, after all, be adults for whom bad news hardly comes as a surprise. And readers must make up their own minds whether or not they believe Hardy's declared wish that his `heart had shrunk as thin` as his `wasting skin`.

It is the fate of every anthology to be criticized. "Why on earth did they include x but leave out y?" If some of our readers are very dissatisfied, they might feel like compiling their own alternative collection. But be warned. There are a few tasks involved. [1]

Given the conflicting views expressed in this anthology, it will be clear that we ourselves could not endorse them all. What we have discovered and now want to share are, quite simply, diverse, eloquent voices on the last stage of life. They are united only in the intensity of their feeling. For, as Lotte Kramer writes in `Stocktaking`:

> And what of passions, hope, the heartbeat lump
>
> Thudding in throat and voice? All still remain.

And Eudora Welty has recalled, in One Writer's Beginnings, how her old mother, when helplessly bedridden and nearly blind, would still recite all the poems she could remember:

"Reciting, her voice took on a resonance and firmness, it rang with the old fervor, with ferocity even. She was teaching me one more, almost her last, lesson: emotions do not grow old. I knew that I would feel as she did, and I do."

Sybil Oldfield and Gwenyth Shaw

---

[1] Funding application forms for local charitable bequests and/or regional funding, e.g. `Awards for All`, need to be filled in. (The Society of Authors, the Poetry Society and the Arts Council do not finance publication costs). And it is usually necessary to convert oneself into a constituted voluntary group before being eligible for any funding. For *every* poem written by someone who died less than seventy years ago there must be an attempt to obtain copyright permission – which may also cost a fee. Who is the copyright holder for each such poet? Consult **WATCH** on Google or check: http://tyler.hrc.utexas.edu/ If nothing comes up, turn to the acknowledgements pages for a wanted poet in other anthologies or the poet's publisher (address in Writers' and Artists' Yearbook). Good luck.

<u>Loving the Living</u>

Ah, love, let us be true
To one another!...

(Matthew Arnold, 1822-1888), *from* `Dover Beach`)

Amo ergo sum. ... Senesco sed amo.
(I love therefore I am ... I am getting old, but I love)

(Ezra Pound, in his early sixties, Canto LXXX)

Think where man's glory most begins and ends,
And say my glory was I had such friends.

(Yeats, `The Municipal Gallery Revisited`, <u>Last Poems</u>)

"Grandson, grandsire, we are equally boy and boy."

(John Crowe Ransom, `Old Man Playing With Children`)

I should have started with the grand-children

(American car sticker)

CHILDREN

My niece, who is six years old, is called "Miss Tortoise";
My daughter of three, - little "Summer Dress."
One is beginning to learn to joke and talk;
The other can already recite poems and songs.
At morning they play clinging about my feet;
At night they sleep pillowed against my dress[1].
Why, children, did you reach the world so late,
Coming to me just when my years are spent?
Young things draw our feelings to them;
Old people easily give their hearts. …

[1] i.e. robe worn by men in traditional China

(Po Chu-I, c. 820 A.D. translated by Arthur Waley)

QUARRELLING

The ancients argued that friendship could never last.
A few old friends, we walk on the mountain's milder slopes,
Discussing their reasons. The wind lifts our coats.
An hour passes, and we find we are shaking our staffs,
We are out of breath. We must have been quarrelling!
Some prophecies, if you listen to them, come true.
Quickly we drop the topic, open the picnic baskets,
And pour the wine. How sad it would be to drink alone!
Someone recites a poem on the sorrow of separation.
It seems the famous sages were not unfailingly right.

(Tao Tschung Yu, ? 18th C. translated by Arthur Waley)

FRIENDSHIP

Such love I cannot analyse;
It does not rest in lips or eyes,
Neither in kisses nor caress.
Partly, I know, it's gentleness

And understanding in one word
Or in brief letters. It's preserved
By trust and by respect and awe.
These are the words I'm feeling for.

Two people, yes, two lasting friends.
The giving comes, the taking ends.
There is no measure for such things,
For this all Nature slows and sings.

(Elizabeth Jennings, 1926-2001, first publ. in Relationships, 1972)

FAREWELL TO A TRAPPIST

This then is love – deep joy that you should be.
Though the world's Gadarene ways astound
I see you and my heart has found
A reason for mankind and an apology.
How slight a chance brings on our destiny!
If death had come when it was due
I should have died as one who never knew,
Without this great content to go with me.
Immured, you may the Unhorizoned view.
In lifelong, solitary thought
Your willing heart out of itself will wreak
The poet's heaven that you seek,
While I, an outer satellite caught,
Dear love, see only you.

(Lucy Boston, 1892-1990, *from* Time is Undone, privately printed 1977

HER GREATEST LOVE

At sixty she's experiencing
the greatest love of her life.

She walks arm in arm with her lover,
the wind ruffles their grey hairs.

Her lover says:
-You have hair like pearls.

Her children say:
-You silly old fool

(Anna Swir, 1909-1984, transl. from Polish by Grazyna Baran
and Margaret Marshment in Fat Like the Sun, 1972)

WISH FOR A YOUNG WIFE

My lizard, my lively writher,
May your limbs never wither,
May the eyes in your face
Survive the green ice
Of envy's mean gaze;
May you live out your life
Without hate, without grief,
And your hair ever blaze,
In the sun, in the sun,
When I am undone,
When I am no one.

(Theodore Roethke, 1908-1963)

from THE ECHOES RETURN SLOW

I look out over the timeless sea
over the head of one, calendar
to time's passing, who is now open
at the last month, her hair wintry.

Am I catalyst of her mettle that,
at my approach, her grimace of pain
turns to a smile? What it is saying is:
`Over love's depths only the surface is wrinkled.`

(R.S.Thomas, 1913-2000, publ. 1988)

UNGEPLANT

Daß ich
viel zu alt bin
für dich
oder daß du
zu jung bist für mich
das sind alle
gewichtige Argumente
die entscheidend wären
in den Lehrwerkstätten
in denen
die aufgeklärteren Menschen
sich ihre berechnete Zukunft
zurechtschneiden
streng nach Maß

UNPLANNED

That I
am much too old
for you
or that you
are too young for me
these are all
weighty arguments
that would be decisive
in the workshops
where
more enlightened people
cut
their calculated futures
strictly to measure

(Erich Fried, 1921-1988, transl. from German by Stuart Hood, *from* Love Poems, 1991)

ABER

Zuerst have ich mich verliebt
in den Glanz deiner Augen

in dein Lachen
in deine Lebensfreude

Jetzt liebe ich auch dein Weinen
und deine Lebensangst
und die Hilflosigkeit
in deinen Augen

Aber gegen die Angst
will ich dir helfen
denn meine Lebensfreude
ist noch immer der Glanz deiner
Augen

BUT

At first I fell in love
with the brightness of your
eyes
with your laugh
with your joy in life

Now I love your weeping too
and your fear of life
and the helplessness
in your eyes

But I will help you
with your fear
for my joy in life
is still the brightness of your
eyes.

(Erich Fried, 1921-1988, transl. from German by Stuart Hood, *from* Love Poems, 1991)

TWO OLD WOMEN

The two of us sit in the doorway,
chatting about our children and grandchildren.
We sink happily
Into our oldwomanhood.

Like two spoons
sinking
into a bowl of hot porridge.

(Anna Swir, 1909-1984, transl. from Polish by Grazyna Baran
and Margaret Marshment in Fat Like the Sun, 1972)

IN PAINSWICK CHURCHYARD

`Is this where people are buried?
I will not let them bury you.`

He picnics among tombs
- pours imaginary tea,
a yew tree his kitchen.

`You will live with me in my house`.
Oh could I believe the living and the dead
inhabit one house under the sky
and you my child run into your future forever.

(Frances Horovitz, 1938-1983, *from* Water over Stone, 1980)

Loving the Dead

When to the sessions of sweet silent thought
I summon up remembrance of things past, …
Then can I drown an eye, unus'd to flow
For precious friends hid in death's dateless night…

(Shakespeare, Sonnet 30)

They are all gone into the world of light!
And I alone sit lingring here;
Their very memory is fair and bright
And my sad thoughts doth clear. …

(Henry Vaughan, Silex Scintillans, 1655)

With regard to the sharpest and most melting sorrow, that which arises from the loss of those whom we have loved with tenderness, it may be observed, that friendship between mortals can be contracted on no other terms, than that one must sometime mourn for the other's death: And this grief will always yield to the survivor one consolation proportionate to his affliction; for the pain, whatever it be, that he himself feels, his friend has escaped.

(Dr. Johnson, The Rambler, No. 17, 15 May, 1750)

…`Tis better to have loved and lost
Than never to have loved at all - …`

(Tennyson, In Memoriam A.H.H. *from* stanza LXXXV)

`… But O for the touch of a vanished hand,
And the sound of a voice that is still. `

(Tennyson, `Break, Break, Break`)

`The dead are often just as living to us as the living are, …`

(Samuel Butler 1835-1902, Notebooks)

IN MOURNING FOR HIS DEAD WIFE

Winter and Spring have come and gone.
Once more Autumn overtakes
Summer. She has returned to
The Hidden Springs. And all the
World separates us forever.
Who will listen to my secrets
Now? Who will I live for now?
I try to do my job at Court,
And reluctantly go through
The motions of duty, and
Take up the tasks I had dropped.
When I come home I can think
Only of her. When I come
In our room I expect to see her.
I catch her shadow on the
Screens and curtains. Her letters
Are the most precious examples
Of calligraphy. Her perfume
Still haunts the bedroom. Her clothes
Still hang in the closet.
She is always alive in
My dreams. I wake with a start.
She vanishes. …

(P'an Yueh P'an, 4th century, transl. by Kenneth Rexroth,
from Love and the Turning Year - One Hundred More Poems from the Chinese, 1970)

THE OLD FAMILIAR FACES

I have had playmates, I have had companions,
In my days of childhood, in my joyful school-days –
All, all are gone, the old familiar faces.

I have been laughing, I have been carousing,
Drinking late, sitting late, with my bosom cronies –
All, all are gone, the old familiar faces. …

Ghost-like I paced round the haunts of my childhood,
Earth seemed a desert I was bound to traverse,
Seeking to find the old familiar faces.

Friend of my bosom, thou more than a brother,
Why were thou not born in my father's dwelling?
So we might talk of the old familiar faces –

How some have died, and some they have left me,
And some are taken from me; all are departed –
All, all are gone, the old familiar faces.

(Charles Lamb, 1774-1834)

EXTEMPORE EFFUSION
UPON THE DEATH OF JAMES HOGG

When first, descending from the moorlands
I saw the Stream of Yarrow glide
Along a bare and open valley,
The Ettrick Shepherd was my guide.

When last along its banks I wandered,
Through groves that had begun to shed
Their golden leaves upon the pathways,
My steps the Border-minstrel led.

The mighty Minstrel breathes no longer,
`Mid mouldering ruins low he lies;
And death upon the braes of Yarrow,
Has closed the Shepherd-poet's eyes.

Nor has the rolling year twice measured,
From sign to sign, its steadfast course,
Since every mortal power of Coleridge
Was frozen at its marvellous source;

The rapt One, of the godlike forehead,
The heaven-eyed creature sleeps in earth;
And Lamb, the frolic and the gentle,
Has vanished from his lonely hearth.

Like clouds that rake the mountain-summits,
Or waves that own no curbing hand,
How fast has brother followed brother,
From sunshine to the sunless land! …

(Wordsworth, 1770-1850, written 1835)

The distance that the dead have gone
Does not at first appear;
Their coming back seems possible
For many an ardent year.

And then that we have followed them
We more than half suspect,
So intimate have we become
With their dear retrospect.

(Emily Dickinson, 1830-1886, written c. 1870)

THE WALK

You did not walk with me
Of late to the hill-top tree
By the gated ways,
As in earlier days;
You were weak and lame,
So you never came,
And I went alone, and I did not mind,
Not thinking of you as left behind.

I walked up there to-day
Just in the former way:
Surveyed around
The familiar ground
By myself again:
What difference, then?
Only that underlying sense
Of the look of a room on returning thence.

(Thomas Hardy, 1840-1928, *from* Satires of Circumstance, 1912-13)

AT CASTLE BOTEREL

As I drive to the junction of lane and highway,
  And the drizzle bedrenches the waggonette,
I look behind at the fading byway,
  And see on its slope, now glistening wet,
    Distinctly yet

Myself and a girlish form benighted
  In dry March weather. We climb the road
Beside a chaise. We had just alighted
  To ease the sturdy pony's load
    When he sighed and slowed.

What we did as we climbed, and what we talked of
  Matters not much, nor to what it led, -
Something that life will not be balked of
  Without reason till hope is dead,
    And feeling fled.

It filled but a minute. But was there ever
  A time of such quality, since or before,
In that hill's story? To one mind never,
  Though it has been climbed, foot-swift, foot-sore,
    By thousands more.

Primaeval rocks form the road's steep border,
  And much have they faced there, first and last,
Of the transitory in Earth's long order;
  But what they record in colour and cast
    Is – that we two passed.

And to me, though Time's unflinching rigour,
  In mindless rote, has ruled from sight
The substance now, one phantom figure
  Remains on the slope, as when that night
    Saw us alight.

I look and see it there, shrinking, shrinking,
  I look back at it amid the rain
For the very last time; for my sand is sinking,
  And I shall traverse old love's domain
      Never again.

(Thomas Hardy, 1840-1928, *from* Satires of Circumstance, 1912-13)

TIME DOES NOT BRING RELIEF

Time does not bring relief; you all have lied
Who told me time would ease me of my pain!
I miss him in the weeping of the rain;
I want him in the shrinking of the tide;
The old snows melt from every mountain-side,
And last year's leaves are smoke in every lane;
But last year's bitter loving must remain
Heaped on my heart, and my old thoughts abide!

There are a hundred places where I fear
To go, - so with his memory they brim!
And entering with relief some quiet place
Where never fell his foot or shone his face
I say, `There is no memory of him here!`
And so stand stricken, so remembering him.

(Edna St. Vincent Millay, 1892-1950)

SEA CANES

Half my friends are dead.
I will make you new ones, said earth.
No, give me them back, as they were, instead,
with faults and all, I cried.

Tonight I can snatch their talk
from the faint surf's drone
through the canes, but I cannot walk

on the moonlit leaves of ocean
down that white road alone,
or float with the dreaming motion

of owls leaving earth's load.
O earth, the number of friends you keep
exceeds those left to be loved.

The sea canes by the cliff flash green and silver;
they were the seraph lances of my faith,
but out of what is lost grows something stronger

that has the rational radiance of stone,
enduring moonlight, further than despair,
strong as the wind, that through the dividing canes
brings those we love before us, as they were,
with faults and all, not nobler, just there.

(Derek Walcott, 1930 -)

ANNIVERSARY

The white rhododendron has come into flower
- one glistening cluster, ripe and virginal
at the same time; it's grown too, in the year
it's been marking the spot – yours, we said,
walking across to it under the apple trees carrying
our glasses of wine - `yes, this is the place` ,
and I think we each did a bit with a trowel.

It wasn't the last word, though – you're here now
in the dusk, laughing somewhere behind me
at what you still had in store for us … but
it's so domestic! Look at me bending down
taking the spoon – a tablespoon (nothing paltry
about this measure) out of the box of … well,
look, it's you, isn't it, this white pile –

why do they call it ashes? My dear, you are grit,
all through; you rattle, you tinkle, as I take
one, two, good spoonfuls of you. It's hilarious
I can see, for the doubled-up ghost of you
over there under the trees, purged of this
heavy stuff, watching me, pointing out
how familiar it is, this kitcheny action, -

after all, most of our time was in kitchens,
talking – or shouting – among cooking and kids,
running a complex show and keeping our spirits up,
eager, or cynical, or frivolous – dog-tired too,
of course. Under the leaves, that white sprinkle
gleams in the darkening garden. Remember the day …
oh to hell with it. I wish you were here.

(Lauris Edmond, 1924-2000, *from* New and Selected Poems, 1992)

PORTRAIT

Speaking always with that
restraint that was itself
an excess. Smiling at us
so as to conceal tears.

Waiting so far ahead
in modesty for us to catch
up as to appear forward.
Apologizing for the time

invested in her, considering
it without interest. Hostess
of life, as unable to help
herself as if she were its guest.

(R.S.Thomas, 1913-2000, from Mass For Hard Times, (1992)
To the Memory of my wife, M.E.Eldridge 1909-1991)

NO TIME

She left me. What voice
colder than the wind
out of the grave said:
`It is over`? Impalpable,
invisible, she comes
to me still, as she would
do, and I at my reading.
There is a tremor
of light, as of a bird crossing
the sun's path, and I look
up in recognition
of a presence in absence.
Not a word, not a sound,
as she goes her way,
but a scent lingering
which is that of time immolating
itself in love's fire.

(R.S.Thomas, 1913-2000, *from* No Truce With the Furies, (1988)
in Collected Later Poems 1988-2000, Bloodaxe Books, 2004)

JEWELS IN MY HAND

I hold dead friends like jewels in my hand
Watching their brilliance gleam against my palm
Turquoise and emerald, jade, a golden band

All ravages of time they can withstand
Like talismans their grace keeps me from harm
I hold dead friends like jewels in my hand

I see them standing in some borderland
Their heads half-turned, waiting for my arm
Turquoise and emerald, jade, a golden band

I'm not afraid they will misunderstand
My turning to them like a magic charm
I hold dead friends like jewels in my hand
Turquoise and emerald, jade, a golden band.

(Sasha Moorsom, 1931-1993, *from* Your Head in Mine, 1994;
written when first treated for terminal cancer)

THE GLASS

To love you in shadow as in the light
is light itself. In subterranean night
you sow the fields with fireflies of delight.

Lanarkshire holds you, under its grim grass.
But I hold what you were, like a bright glass
I carry brimming through the darkening pass.

(Edwin Morgan, 1920 - :`The Glass` is about a much loved person who died in 1978 and was buried on a cold, bleak day in a Lanarkshire cemetery. The poem was written about twenty years later, and published in Virtual and Other Realities, 1997 ...the persistence of memory can be extremely vivid and fruitful, a dead person can be both virtual and real`. Poem for the Day (Two), 2005)

CEARA

Her Love
Her Beauty
Her Laughter
They will never fade

(Headstone for Ceara Bath, Berwick Churchyard, East Sussex)

Being Loved

…Say I'm weary, say I'm sad,
Say that health and wealth have miss'd me,
Say I'm growing old, but add
Jenny kiss'd me.

(Leigh Hunt 1784-1859; *from* 'Jenny Kiss'd Me')

And did you get what
you wanted from this life, even so?
I did.
And what did you want?
To call myself beloved, to feel myself
beloved on the earth.

(Raymond Carver 1938-1988; his last poem)

TO MY MOTHER

Most near, most dear, most loved and most far,
Under the window where I often found her
Sitting as huge as Asia, seismic with laughter,
Gin and chicken helpless in her Irish hand,
Irresistible as Rabelais, but most tender for
The lame dogs and hurt birds that surround her, -
She is a procession no one can follow after
But be like a little dog following a brass band.

She will not glance up at the bomber, or condescend
To drop her gin and scuttle to a cellar,
But lean on the mahogany table like a mountain
Whom only faith can move, and so I send
O all my faith, and all my love to tell her
That she will move from mourning into morning.

(George Barker, 1913-1991)

IN MEMORY OF MY MOTHER

I do not think of you lying in the wet clay
Of a Monaghan graveyard; I see
You walking down a lane among the poplars
On your way to the station, or happily

Going to second Mass on a summer Sunday –
You meet me and you say:
`Don't forget to see about the cattle -`
Among your earthiest words the angels stray.

And I think of you walking along a headland
Of green oats in June,
So full of repose, so rich with life –
And I see us meeting at the end of a town

On a fair day by accident, after
The bargains are all made and we can walk
Together through the shops and stalls and markets
Free in the oriental streets of thought.

O you are not lying in the wet clay,
For it is a harvest evening now and we
Are piling up the ricks against the moonlight
And you smile up at us – eternally.

(Patrick Kavanagh, 1904-1967)

REFERENCE BACK

That was a pretty one, I heard you call
From the unsatisfactory hall
To the unsatisfactory room where I
Played record after record, idly,
Wasting my time at home, that you
Looked so much forward to.

Oliver's *Riverside Blues*, it was. And now
I shall, I suppose, always remember how
The flock of notes those antique Negroes blew
Out of Chicago air into
A huge remembering pre-electric horn
The year after I was born
Three decades later made this sudden bridge
From your unsatisfactory age
To my unsatisfactory prime.

Truly, though our element is time,
We are not suited to the long perspectives
Open at each instant of our lives.
They link us to our losses: worse,
They show us what we have as it once was,
Blindingly undiminished, just as though
By acting differently we could have kept it so.

(Philip Larkin, 1922-1985)

MARY GRAVELY JONES

We had no petnames, no diminutives for you,
always the formal guest under my father's roof:
you were "Grandmother Jones" and you visited rarely.
I see you walking up and down the garden,
restless, southern-accented, reserved, you did not seem
my mother's mother or anyone's grandmother.
You were Mary, widow of William, and no matriarch,
yet smoldering to the end with frustrate life,
ideas nobody listened to, least of all my father.
One summer night you sat with my sister and me
in the wooden glider long after twilight,
holding us there with streams of pent-up words.
You could quote every poet I had ever heard of,
had read *The Opium Eater*, Amiel and Bernard Shaw,
your green eyes looked clenched against opposition.
You married straight out of the convent school,
your background was country, you left an unperformed
typescript of a play about Burr and Hamilton,
you were impotent and brilliant, no one cared
about your mind, you might have ended
elsewhere than in that glider
reciting your unwritten novels to the children.

(Adrienne Rich, 1929 - *from* 'Grandmothers' in A Wild Patience Has Taken Me This Far, Poems 1979-1981)

STATIONS UNDERGROUND

1. Fanfare

(for Winifrid Fanthorpe, born 5 February 1895, died 13 November 1978)

You, in the old photographs, are always
The one with the melancholy half-smile, the one
Who couldn't quite relax into the joke.

My extrovert dog of a father,
With his ragtime blazer and his swimming togs
Tucked like a swiss roll under his arm,
Strides in his youth towards us down some esplanade,

Happy as Larry. You, on his other arm,
Are anxious about the weather forecast,
His overdraft, or early closing day.

You were good at predicting failure: marriages
Turned out wrong because you said they would.
You knew the rotations of armistice and war,
Watched politicians' fates with gloomy approval.

All your life you lived in a minefield,
And were pleased, in a quiet way, when mines
Exploded. You never actually said
I told you so, but we could tell you meant it.

Crisis was your element. You kept your funny stories,
Your music-hall songs for doodlebug and blitz-nights.
In the next cubicle, after a car-crash, I heard you
Amusing the nurses with your trench wit through the blood.

Magic alerted you. Green, knives and ladders
Will always scare me through your tabus.
Your nightmare was Christmas; so much organised
Compulsory whoopee to be got through.

You always had some stratagems for making
Happiness keep its distance. Disaster
Was what you planned for. You always
Had hoarded loaves or candles up your sleeve.

Houses crumbled around your ears, taps leaked,
Electric light bulbs went out all over England,
Because for you homes were only provisional,
Bivouacs on the stony mountain of living.

You were best at friendship with chars, gipsies,
Or very far-off foreigners. Well-meaning neighbours
Were dangerous because they lived near.

Me too you managed best at a distance. On the landline
From your dugout to mine, your nightly
Pass, friend was really often quite jovial.

You were the lonely figure in the doorway
Waving goodbye in the cold, going back to a sink-full
Of crockery dirtied by those you loved. We
Left you behind to deal with our crusts and gristle.

I know why you chose now to die. You foresaw
Us approaching the Delectable Mountains,
And didn't feel up to all the cheers and mafficking.

But how, dearest, will even you retain your
Special brand of hard-bitten stoicism
Among the halleluyas of the triumphant dead?

(UA Fanthorpe, 1929- *from* Standing To, 1982)

HANDBAG

My mother's old leather handbag,
Crowded with letters she carried
All through the war. The smell
Of my mother's handbag: mints
And lipstick and Coty powder.
The look of those letters, softened
And worn at the edges, opened,
Read, and refolded so often.
Letters from my father. Odour
Of leather and powder, which ever
Since then has meant womanliness,
And love, and anguish, and war.

(Ruth Fainlight, 1931- *from* Fifteen to Infinity, 1983)

PRAISE SONG FOR MY MOTHER

You were
water to me
deep and bold and fathoming

You were
moon's eye to me
pull and grained and mantling

You were
sunrise to me
rise and warm and streaming

You were
the fishes red gill to me
the flame tree's spread to me
the crab's leg/ the fried plantain smell
replenishing replenishing

Go to your wide futures, you said

(Grace Nichols, 1950 - *from* The Fat Black Woman's Poems, 1984)

A CALL

`Hold on,` she said, `I'll just run out and get him.
The weather here's so good, he took the chance
To do a bit of weeding.` So I saw him
Down on his hands and knees beside the leek rig,
Touching, inspecting, separating one
Stalk from the other, gently pulling up
Everything not tapered, frail and leafless,
Pleased to feel each little weed-root break,
But rueful also …

Then found myself listening to
The amplified grave ticking of hall clocks
Where the phone lay unattended in a calm
Of mirror glass and sunstruck pendulums …

And found myself then thinking: if it were nowadays,
This is how Death would summon Everyman.

Next thing he spoke and I nearly said I loved him.

(Seamus Heaney, 1939-, *from* The Spirit Level, 1996)

CATTLE IN MIST

A postcard from my father's childhood –
the one nobody photographed or painted;
the one we never had, my sister and I.
Such feeble daughters – couldn't milk a cow
(watched it now and then, but no one taught us).
How could we hold our heads up, having never
pressed them into the warm flank of a beast
and lured the milk down? His, hiss, in a bucket:
routine, that's all. Not ours. That one missed us.

His later childhood, I should say;
not his second childhood – that he evaded
by dying – and his first was Manchester.
But out there in the bush, from the age of ten,
in charge of milking, rounding up the herd,
combing the misty fringes of the forest
(as he would have had to learn not to call it)
at dawn, and again after school, for stragglers;
cursing them; bailing them up; it was no childhood.

A talent-spotting teacher saved him.
The small neat smiling boy (I'm guessing)
evolved into a small neat professor.
He could have spent his life wreathed in cow-breath,
a slave to endlessly refilling udders,
companion of heifers, midwife at their calvings,
judicious pronouncer on milk-yields and mastitis,
survivor of the bull he bipped on the nose
(`Tell us again, Daddy!`) as it charged him.

All his cattle: I drive them back
into the mist, into the dawn haze
where they can look romantic; where they must
have wandered now for sixty or seventy years.
Off they go, then, tripping over the tree-roots,
pulling up short to lip at a tasty twig,
bumping into each other, stumbling off again
into the bush. He never much liked them.
He'll never need to rustle them back again.

(Fleur Adcock, 1934 - from Poems 1960-2000)

INTENSIVE CARE

Your voice silenced by tubes,
the mute, continual cough lifts you awake.
I stroke your hair; you stare at me,
eyes remote, tearless.

You write, `I'm hungry`,
I watch each breath
sucked in between your ribs,
beg for you.

You lie as if in state,
too dignified.
If I thought you were leaving me
from this white room

with only plastic pillows for your journey
I would cram your hands with anemones,
snatch out the catheters, enfold you,
run with you to where the band is playing.

But now, as my hands
make shadow creatures on the wall,
I read your lips: `rhinoceros`,
know I have you still.

(Carole Satyamurti, 1939 -, *from* Broken Moon, 1987)

FULL MOON WITH MY GRANDMOTHER

Because your time s short, we draw it out,
like this early summer evening by the sea,
as we prolong our talk, delay the hour I leave,
though now the pier is lit with electric light,
or a winter midnight, when we stood and stared
at the full moon on the water, like a path
to the other side of life. I wanted to ask,
`Where will it take you? Will I see you there? `

The stars above are already burnt and gone
by the time we spy them, which goes to prove
a memory of dust and ashes lingers on,
and if we choose to, we may call this love.
As you sail alone to another shore, know
my footsteps in the sand are here. I follow.

(Sarah Wardle, 1969 - , *from* Fields Away, 2003)

CLIMBING MY GRANDFATHER

I decide to do it free, without a rope or net.
First, the old brogues, dusty and cracked;
an easy scramble onto his trousers,
pushing into the weave, trying to get a grip.
By the overhanging shirt I change
direction, traverse along his belt
to an earth-stained hand. The nails
are splintered and give good purchase,
the skin of his finger is smooth and thick
like warm ice. On his arm I discover
the glassy ridge of a scar, place my feet
gently in the old stitches and move on.
At his still firm shoulder, I rest for a while
in the shade, not looking down,
for climbing has its dangers, then pull
myself up the loose skin of his neck
to a smiling mouth to drink among teeth.
Refreshed, I cross the screed cheek,
to stare into his brown eyes, watch a pupil
slowly open and close. Then up over
the forehead, the wrinkles well-spaced
and easy, to his thick hair (soft and white
at this altitude), reaching for the summit,
where gasping for breath I can only lie
watching clouds and birds circle,
feeling his heat, knowing the slow pulse of his good heart.

(Andrew Waterhouse, 1958-2001, *from* In, 2000)

WHEN IN THE WORLD

When you were with me in the world
we inhabited, the only one,
it seemed I had all the time
to muse on my father's flight out,
a tough old ball kicked out of touch
in a moment. With you still
there, I'd have time to catch the speed
of my father's throw, his people,
his work, his talk, bright-eyed,
impatient, charmer repentant, self on the go.

To say you've gone. You too?
The two who were one because
always the two. What do I say
now, of his death: that it propped you
in astonished, blinded anguish.
How you said after, you `chose to live`,
that you had your own `mission`,
to see, to help, what would become
of us, our children, how live,
how flourish, how you could help.

Poor mother, how could you help
each day multiplying into sleep,
your good sense, even your fatwa –
the book, the book, it has to be written!
You like a little animal hunched
Dozing on the old yellow sofa,
but glad always to charm the guest,
the guest of your house, welcomed
with the open smile of decades.
Then my father dreamed of, desperado ghost,
for where so sadly did he wander
in forgotten hospital corridors, forgotten,
and how could you help him?

The last August, our birthdays, both –
you sat down, hunched,
our Mrs. Tiggiwinkle , on the bed
I'd christened your daybed, where
between tall windows you slept
the summer afternoons, your garden green.
One morning, such stiff pain from
upstairs bed to downstairs bed, you
slowly sat, without looking at me:
`What's it for?` All you could say.
A year on, facing no hope, no death.

I couldn't bear to know.
What you'd always feared, and I
also, the unuseful quiet: the void.
Never in both your two lives
did you let that sneaky void,
that snag in the good gardener's working
day, that small wizened worm,
get you. I hastily talked. You turned,
lay down, finished the painful
movement, without comment.

(Judith Kazantzis, 1942 - , *from* Just After Midnight, 2004)

THE PHOTOGRAPH

The telephone shrills through the silences
to ask what you're doing and how you are
my tone is cheerful and solicitous
making sure all's well at your end
noising my busyness into your ear
stories of today and yesterday
journeys ended and journeys to come
and what I say is what I always say
and what I want to say I never say.

Sharp in the sepia of a family group
Grandma's brow smooth beneath her weight of hair
Grandpa's eyes young, his moustache waxed and twirled,
your hand rests on your brother's head
and as you welcome the camera
in Alice gaze of expectation
I see familiar eyes that don't see me
looking beyond the limits of my love
and will not tell you how I love that child
and cannot tell you how she breaks my heart.

(Barbara Hardy, 1925 - , *from* The Yellow Gospel, 2006)

BEARHUGS

Whenever my sons call round we hug each other.
Bearhugs. Both bigger than me and stronger
They lift me off my feet, crushing the life out of me.

They smell of oil paint and aftershave, of beer
Sometimes and tobacco, and of women
Whose memory they seem reluctant to wash away.

They haven't lived with me for years,
Since they were tiny, and each visit
Is an assessment, a reassurance of love unspoken.

I look for some resemblance to my family.
Seize on an expression, a lifted eyebrow,
A tilt of the head, but cannot see myself.

Though like each other, they are not like me.
But I can see in them something of my father.
Uncles, home on leave during the war.

At three or four, I loved those straightbacked men
Towering above me, smiling and confident.
The whole world before them. Or so it seemed.

I look at my boys, slouched in armchairs
They have outgrown. Imagine Tom in army uniform
And Finn in air force blue. Time is up.

Bearhugs. They lift me off my feet
And fifty years fall away. One son
After another, crushing the life into me.

(Roger McGough, 1937- , *from* Selected Poems, 2006)

POSTCARD TO WOLVERCOTE CEMETERY

For Margaret Amosu 1920 - 2005

I came here seeking Africa, but it is you I find,
stepping weightless beside me through the galleries,
far from your quiet cell on the other side of the sea.

You watch me, pensive, in front of the delicate ivory comb,
whorled and scored; we gaze at the dull gold crocodile,
ancient dirt tamped deep between his scales.

A pipe bowl stretches into a naked, long-limbed girl
for the smoker's drinking fellows to envy, his rough palm to cherish.
I hear your longing whispering hopeless down the hall.

The last time I was in this place was with you, seeing
with your eyes. But now I am blind like the Benin door,
its thirty eyelids heavy with duty and your new silence.

I find your going in words, memory, movement, all fading
my life muffled by your absence, hanging still as museum air.
Come back. Or, I beg you, go on ahead.

(Akwe Amosu, 1960 - , *National Museum of African Art*, Cape Town, February, 2006)

Remembering

There was a time when meadow, grove, and stream,
The earth, and every common sight,
To me did seem
Apparell'd in celestial light,
The glory and the freshness of a dream. …

(Wordsworth, 1770-1850) Ode, lines written March, 1802)

…The days gone by
Come back upon me from the dawn almost
Of life: the hiding-places of my power
Seem open; I approach, and then they close;
I see by glimpses now; when age comes on,
May scarcely see at all, …

(Wordsworth, 1770-1850, The Prelude, Book XI, c. 1805)

Oft in the stilly night
Ere slumber's chain has bound me,
Fond Memory brings the light
Of other days around me …

(Thomas. Moore, 1779-1852 `The Light of Other Days`)

I remember, I remember
The house where I was born, …

(Thomas Hood, 1799-1845 `Past and Present`)

from FIVE POEMS ON RETURNING TO LIVE IN THE COUNTRY

No.4

It is long since I wandered among hills and marshes,
Delighting to roam the forest wilds.
But now I take my nephews by the hand,
Push through the bushes and find a ruined town.
We wander up and down among the grave-mounds,
And think of the men who dwelt here long ago.
Traces of wells and hearth-stones still remain,
And rotting stumps of mulberry and bamboo.
I ask a man who's gathering firewood there
What happened to the people of this place.
The firewood-gatherer turns to me and says:
`They're dead and gone, and that's the end of them. `
`Market and court change in a generation.` ...

(T'ao Chi'en, 365-427 A.D, *from* J.D.Frodsham, An Anthology of Chinese Verse, Oxford, Clarendon Press, 1967)

REMEMBRANCES

Summer's pleasures they are gone like to visions every one
And the cloudy days of autumn and of winter cometh on
I tried to call them back but unbidden they are gone
Far away from heart and eye and for ever faraway
Dear heart and can it be that such raptures meet decay
I thought them all eternal when by Langley bush I lay
I thought them joys eternal when I used to shout and play
On its banks at clink and bandy chock and taw and ducking stone
Where silence sitteth now on the wild heath as her own
Like a ruin of the past all alone

When I used to lye and sing by old eastwell's boiling spring
When I used to tie the willow boughs together for a swing
And fish with crooked pins and thread and never catch a thing
With heart just like a feather – now as heavy as a stone –
When beneath old lea close oak I the bottom branches broke
To make our harvest cart like so many working folk
And then to cut a straw at the brook to have a soak
O I never dreamed of parting or that trouble had a sting
Or that pleasures like a flock of birds would ever take to wing
Leaving nothing but a little naked spring

When jumping time away on old crossberry way
And eating awes like sugar plums ere they had lost the may
And skipping like a leveret before the peep of day
On the rolly poly up and down of pleasant Swordy Well
When in round oak's narrow lane as the South got black again
We sought the hollow ash that was shelter from the rain
With our pockets full of pease we had stolen from the grain
How delicious was the dinner time on such a showery day
O words are poor receipts for what time hath stole away
The ancient pulpit trees and the play

When for school o'er little field with its brook and wooden brig
Where I swaggered like a man though I was not half so big
While I held my little plough though 'twas but a willow twig
And drove my team along made of nothing but a name
'Gee hep' and 'hoit' and 'woi' – O I never call to mind
Those pleasant names of places but I leave a sigh behind
While I see the little mouldiwarps hang sweeing to the wind
On the only aged willow that in all the field remains
And nature hides her face while they're sweeing in their chains
And in a silent murmuring complains

Here was commons for their hills where they seek for freedom still
Though every common's gone and though traps are set to kill
The little homeless miners – O it turns my bosom chill
When I think of old `sneap green`, puddock's nook, and hilly snow
Where bramble bushes grew and the daisey gemmed in dew
And the hills of silken grass like to cushions on the view

Where we threw the pismire crumbs when we'd nothing else to do
All leveled like a desert by the never-weary plough
All banished like the sun where that cloud is passing now
And settled here for ever on its brow

O I never thought that joys would run away from boys
Or that boys should change their minds and forsake mid-summer joys
But alack I never dreamed that the world had other toys
To petrify first feelings, like the fable, into stone
Till I found the pleasure past and a winter come at last
Then the fields were sudden bare and the sky got overcast
And boyhood's pleasing haunts like a blossom in the blast
Was shrivelled to a withered weed and trampled down and done
Till vanished was the morning spring and set the summer sun
And winter fought her battle-strife and won

By Langley bush I roam but the bush hath left its hill
On cowper green I stray, 'tis a desert strange and chill
And spreading lea close oak ere decay had penned its will
To the axe of the spoiler and self-interest fell a prey
And crossberry way and old round oak's narrow lane
With its hollow trees like pulpits I shall never see again,
Inclosure like a Buonaparte let not a thing remain
It levelled every bush and tree and levelled every hill
And hung the moles for traitors –though the brook is running still
It runs a naked stream cold and chill

O had I known as then joy had left the paths of men
I had watched her night and day besure, and never slept agen
And when she turned to go O I'd caught her mantle hem
And wooed her like a lover by my lonely side to stay
Aye, knelt and worshiped on, as love in beauty's bower
And clung upon her smiles as a bee upon a flower
And gave her heart my poesys all cropt in a sunny hour
As keepsakes and pledges all to never fade away
But love never heeded to treasure up the may
So it went the common road to decay

(John Clare, 1793-1864)

FRIENDS BEYOND

William Dewy, Tranter Reuben, Farmer Ledlow late at plough
Robert's kin, and John's and Ned's,
And the Squire, and Lady Susan, lie in Mellstock churchyard now!

`Gone, ` I call them, gone for good, that group of local hearts and heads;
Yet at mothy curfew-tide,
And at midnight when the noon-heat breathes it back from walls and leads,

They've a way of whispering to me – fellow-wight who yet abide –
In the muted, measured note
Of a ripple under archways, or a lone cave's stillicide: …

`No more need we corn and clothing, feel of old terrestrial stress;
Chill detraction stirs no sigh;
Fear of death has even bygone us: death gave all that we possess. `

W.D. - `Ye mid burn the old bass-viol that I set such value by. `
Squire. - `You may hold the manse in fee,
You may wed my spouse. May let my children's memory of me die. `

Lady S. - `You may have my rich brocades, my laces; take each household key;
Ransack coffer, desk, bureau;
Quiz the few poor treasures hid there, con the letters kept by me. `

Far.- `Ye mid zell my favourite heifer, ye mid let the charlock grow,
Foul the grinterns, give up thrift.
Far. Wife. - `If ye break my best blue china, children, I shan't care or ho. `

All. - `We've no wish to hear the tidings, how the people's fortunes shift;
What your daily doings are;
Who are wedded, born, divided; if your lives beat slow or swift.

`Curious not the least are we if our intents you make or mar,
If you quire to our old tune,
If the City stage still passes, if the weirs still roar afar. `

- Thus with very gods' composure, freed those crosses late and soon
Which, in life, the Trine allow
(Why, none witteth), and ignoring all that haps beneath the moon,

William Dewy, Tranter Reuben, Farmer Ledlow late at plough,
Robert's kin, and John's, and Ned's,
And the Squire, and Lady Susan, murmur mildly to me now.

(Thomas Hardy, 1840-1928, *from* Wessex Poems, before 1898)

THE SELF-UNSEEING

Here is the ancient floor,
Footworn and hollowed and thin,
Here was the former door
Where the dead feet walked in.

She sat here in the chair,
Smiling into the fire;
He who played stood there,
Bowing it higher and higher.

Childlike, I danced in a dream
Blessings emblazoned that day;
Everything glowed with a gleam;
Yet we were looking away!

(Thomas Hardy, 1840-1928, before 1901)

THE SECRETS OF THE OLD

I have old women's secrets now
That had those of the young;
Madge tells me what I dared not think
When my blood was strong,
And what had drowned a lover once
Sounds like an old song.

Though Margery is stricken dumb
If thrown in Madge's way,
We three make up a solitude;
For none alive to-day
Can know the stories that we know
Or say the things we say;

How such a man pleased women most
Of all that are gone,
How such a pair loved many years
And such a pair but one,
Stories of the bed of straw
Or the bed of down.

(Yeats, 1865-1939, *from* 'A Man Young and Old', The Tower, 1928)

ACQUAINTED WITH THE NIGHT

I have been one acquainted with the night.
I have walked out in rain – and back in rain.
I have outwalked the furthest city light.

I have looked down the saddest city lane.
I have passed by the watchman on his beat
And dropped my eyes, unwilling to explain.

I have stood still and stopped the sound of feet
When far away an interrupted cry
Came over houses from another street,

But not to call me back or say goodbye;
And further still at an unearthly height,
One luminary clock against the sky
Proclaimed the time was neither wrong nor right.
I have been one acquainted with the night.

(Robert Frost, 1874-1963, *from* West-Running Brook, [1925?])

BEAUTIFUL LOFTY THINGS

Beautiful lofty things: O'Leary's noble head;
My father upon the Abbey stage, before him a raging crowd:
`This land of Saints,` and then as the applause died out,
`Of plaster Saints`; his beautiful mischievous head thrown
back.
Standish O'Grady supporting himself between the tables
Speaking to a drunken audience high nonsensical words;
Augusta Gregory seated at her great ormolu table,
Her eightieth winter approaching: `Yesterday he
threatened my life.
I told him that nightly from six to seven I sat at this table,
The blinds drawn up`; Maud Gonne at Howth station
waiting a train,
Pallas Athene in that straight back and arrogant head:
All the Olympians; a thing never known again.

(Yeats, 1865-1939, publ. 1935)

SOAP SUDS

This brand of soap has the same smell as once in the big
House he visited when he was eight; the walls of the bathroom open
To reveal a lawn where a great yellow ball rolls back through a hoop
To rest at the head of a mallet held in the hands of a child.

And these were the joys of that house: a tower with a telescope,
Two great faded globes, one of the earth, one of the stars;
A stuffed black dog in the hall; a walled garden with bees;
A rabbit warren; a rockery ; a vine under glass; the sea.

To which he has now returned. The day of course is fine
And a grown-up voice cries Play! The mallet slowly swings,
Then crack, a great gong booms from the dog-dark hall and the ball
Skims forward through the hoop and then through the next and then

Through hoops where no hoops were and each dissolves in turn
And the grass has grown head-high and an angry voice cries Play!
But the ball is lost and the mallet slipped long since from the hands
Under the running tap that are not the hands of a child.

(Louis MacNeice, 1907-1963)

OLD FRIENDS

The sky widens to Cornwall. A sense of sea
  Hangs in the lichenous branches
    and still there's light.
The road from its tunnel of blackthorn rises free
          To a final height,

And over the west is glowing a mackerel sky
  Whose opal fleece has faded to purple pink.
In this hour of the late-lit, listening evening, why
          Do my spirits sink?

The tide is high and a sleepy Atlantic sends
  Exploring ripple on ripple down Polzeath shore,
And the gathering dark is full of the thought of friends
    I shall see no more.

Where is Anne Channel who loved this place the best,
  With her tense blue eyes and her shopping-bag
   falling apart
And her racy gossip and nineteen-twenty zest,
    And that warmth of heart?

Where's Roland, easing his most unwieldy car
  With its load of golf-clubs, backwards into the lane?
Where Kathleen Stokes with her Sealyhams? There's
   Doom Bar;
    Bray Hill shows plain;

For this is the turn, and the well-known trees
   draw near;
  On the road their pattern in moonlight fades
   and swells:
As the engine stops, from two miles off I hear
    St Minver bells.

What a host of stars in a wideness still and deep:
  What a host of souls, as a motor-bike whines away
And the silver snake of the estuary curls to sleep
    In Daymer Bay.

Are they one with the Celtic saints
   and the years between?
  Can they see the moonlit pools
   where ribbonweed drifts?
As I reach our hill I am part of a sea unseen -
    The oppression lifts.

(John Betjeman 1906-1984, first published 1966)

THE TUNE THE OLD COW DIED OF

`The tune the old cow died of,`
My grandmother used to say
When my uncle played the flute.
She hadn't seen a cow for many a day,
Shut in by slate
Walls that bound her
To scullery and yard and soot-
Blackened flowerpots and hart's-
tongue fern.
She watched her fourteen sons grow up around her
In a back street,
Blocked at one end by crags of slag,
Barred at the other by the railway goods-yard gate.
The toot of the flute
Piped to a parish where never cow could earn
Her keep – acres of brick
With telegraph poles and chimneys reared up thick
As ricks in a harvest field.
My grandmother remembered
Another landscape where the cattle
Waded halfway to the knees
In swish of buttercup and yellow rattle,
And un-shorn, parasite-tormented sheep
Flopped down like grey bolsters in the shade of trees,
Was the whine of a hound
In the out-of-hunting-season summer,
Or the cheep of wide-beaked, new-hatched starlings,
Or the humdrum hum of the bees.

Then
A cow meant milk, meant cheese, meant money,
And when a cow died
With foot-and-mouth or wandered out on the marshes
And drowned at the high tide,
The children went without whatever their father had promised.
When she was a girl
There was nothing funny,
My grandmother said,
About the death of a cow,
And it isn't funny now
To millions hungrier even than she was then.
So when the babies cried
One after each other for over fourteen years,
Or the flute squeaked at her ears,
Or the council fire-alarm let off a scream
Like steam out of a kettle and the whole mad town
Seemed fit to blow its lid off – she could find
No words to ease her mind
Like those remembered from her childhood fears:
`The tune the old cow died of`.`

(Norman Nicholson, 1914-1987)

ON SHUTTING THE DOOR

Often, when I leave home,
I think of you,
How you'd have shut the door
That last time
They fetched you out at dawn.

What fears would prophesy,
What intimations
Could foretell the terrors
Of those plains,
The herding into ash?

Or maybe, you looked round
As if before
A holiday, leaving
No trace of dust
No crumbs for pests, no moths

In cupboards, carpets;
Covered the chairs
The settee from the glare
Of light and sun,
Turned off the water, gas …

BARRICADES

She is wailing in the archaic
German of her childhood
Across continents of cinders
Unthought of by doctors and
nurses.

In her long-ago house
She sends us down to the cellar
Through a coal-dark door
To fetch a bottle of lemonade .

She is waiting with certainty
For her dead husband's arrival
But weeps because `too many
Stones on the path -
he can't cross the stones.`

Her room is my prison.
My shame is my fear
Of her plundered world
I refuse to enter.

(Lotte Kramer, 1923 - , a *Kindertransport* German Jewish child refugee to Britain in 1939,
from The Shoemaker's Wife, 1987 and The Destruction of Trees, 1994)

1959

Never go back. I knew that. Never years after
not even in sunlight in winter in winter's sunlit cold
go back to such streets and remember on every corner
the young lived here and now; these young are dead or old.

So I went back: webfoot across the traffic
contrary against crowds I went back in the gloom
head bent in a drizzle of autumn and turned for comfort
into a bar was a bar was more like a tomb

or a tidy morgue with a licence now open for custom,
no matter how many, the size or the sex, could lie
stiffly out stretched on those pink formica tables
no ghost could unbend at that counter: no more could I.

So where? At this unbewitching hour when shops draw shutters
and kitchens stir under halflit restaurants
and the lounger tires of the ads in the evening papers
and the sons and daughters of music tire of recorded song.

But the long straight street in the thin rain.
Demolitions dilapidations; scaffolding girders hoardings;
landmarks shored
against these ruins. Bertorelli, Tiranti;
the church it seems and the pawnshop are not to be restored.

And so? A way a lone a last the
long loved street to watch the windless fall
of plane leaves clutch the pavements like severed swans feet
is this to be for a sign? this all

back, here, now, in the street; the houses like minipalazzi
a canal has dried up on; no footstep on a stair,
those stony stairs; no light in a third floor window
on this street where everything happened: a marriage a birth a war. …

(Sean Rafferty, 1909-1993 *from* Collected Poems, 1995)

FRANCIS AT MADRON

(i)

A dead end, so it seemed, not worth the walk;
That broad green track with, on its left, a swamp,
Tussocky grass, blackthorn and alder thickets,
Lichen encrustments, mosses, seepage, mud;
And, in the swamp, the trampled spring, a cleft
With its few tumbled stones, its tasselled tree,
Limp, sodden strips of cloth tied to each twig;
Fifty yards on, the ruined baptistery,
Its corbelled cistern, water channel, bench,
And a bare altar stone; and then, a barbed-wire fence.

(ii)

`Remember me at Madron`, Francis said
Just days before he died; then smiled at me:
`That is, whenever you decide to go.
There isn't much to see: a ruin and a well.
But look and listen and be still. And take your boots.
It's wet.` It always is. Why do I come?
I didn't; not for weeks, for months, for years;
Wouldn't confront this chosen trysting place;
Shied off, afraid. Closure, they prattle, closure;
Not closure but continuance, my need.

(iii)

And so I came to Madron, late and questioningly.
There wasn't much to see – and it was wet.
`We need new eyes`, Francis would say, `new ears…`
But why come here? What did he hope I'd find?
The rags? Remember `Tie it well and let it go`?
I have his *Herbert* with that riddling proverb marked
And *nexus rerum* marked in another book:
The ties that bind the worlds? The knottedness of things?
The cistern's seaward waters promising a world
Remade? The well – its shadowy holiness?
The pulse of being in the spring itself …
Unanswered questions. Stillness. Murmurings.

(iv)

Always the whispering water-sound, seepings
Becoming tricklings, quickening to a flow ...
The bleached rags stirring in the breath of air ...
The cool clear running in the baptistery ...
The glow of light in early evening rain ...
I come here still: again again again

(Rodney Hillman, 1936 - *from* Heartland, 2006)

Reflecting

Were it to live againe, it should be as I have already lived. … I have seene the leaves, the blossomes, and the fruit; and now see the drooping and withering of it. Happily, because naturally.

(Florio's translation of Montaigne`s Essay `Of Repenting`. 1603)

"What is the price of Experience? Do men buy it for a song?
Or wisdom for a dance in the street? No, it is bought with the price
Of all that a man hath, his house, his wife, his children. ..."

(Blake, Vala, or The Four Zoas, Night the Second. 1795-1804)

… It was not (to start again) what one had expected.
What was to be the value of the long looked forward to,
Long hoped for calm, the autumnal serenity
And the wisdom of age? Had they deceived us
Or deceived themselves, the quiet-voiced elders, …
There is, it seems to us,
At best, only a limited value
In the knowledge derived from experience.
The knowledge imposes a pattern, and falsifies,
For the pattern is new in every moment
And every moment is a new and shocking
Valuation of all we have been. …
The only wisdom we can hope to acquire
Is the wisdom of humility: …

(T.S.Eliot, 1888-1965, *from* `East Coker`, 1940, publ. in Four Quartets, 1944)

Older, and no wiser,
I sit in the sun
With understanding
That's always on the edge
Nearing its conclusions,
Always getting closer
But never reaching
What I want to know….

(Douglas Dunn, *from* `On Whether Loneliness Has a Beginning` in The Year's Afternoon, 2000)

ON BEING SIXTY

Addressed to Liu Meng – te, who had asked for a poem. He was the same age as Po Chu-i.

Between thirty and forty, one is distracted by the Five Lusts;
Between seventy and eighty, one is prey to a hundred diseases.
But from fifty to sixty one is free from all ills;
Calm and still – the heart enjoys rest.
I have put behind me Love and Greed; I have done with Profit and Fame; …

(Po Chu-I, 772-846 transl. Arthur Waley)

SONNET 66

Tir'd with all these for restful death I cry, -
As to behold Desert a beggar born,
And needy Nothing trimm'd in jollity,.
And purest Faith unhappily forsworn,
And gilded Honour shamefully misplac'd,
And maiden Virtue rudely strumpeted,
And right Perfection wrongfully disgrac'd,
And Strength by limping Sway disabl`ed,
And Art made tongue-tied by Authority,
And Folly, Doctor-like, controlling Skill,
And simple Truth miscall'd Simplicity.
And captive Good attending captain Ill:
Tir'd with all these, from these would I be gone –
Save that, to die, I leave my love alone.

(Shakespeare 1564-1616, first publ. 1609)

I stepped from plank to plank,
A slow and cautious way;
The stars about my head I felt,
About my feet the sea.

I knew not but the next
Would be my final inch.
This gave me that precarious gait
Some call experience.

(Emily Dickinson, c.1864)

… I am content to live it all again
And yet again, if it be life to pitch
Into the frog-spawn of a blind man's ditch,
A blind man battering blind men;
Or into that most fecund ditch of all,
The folly that man does
Or must suffer, if he woos
A proud woman not kindred of his soul.

I am content to follow to its source
Every event in action or in thought;
Measure the lot; forgive myself the lot!
When such as I cast out remorse
So great a sweetness flows into the breast
We must laugh and we must sing,
We are blest by everything,
Everything we look upon is blest.

(W.B. Yeats, 1870-1939, *from* `A Dialogue of Self and Soul` in The Winding Stair, 1933)

… Home is where one starts from. As we grow older
The world becomes stranger, the pattern more complicated
Of dead and living. Not the intense moment
Isolated, with no before and after,
But a lifetime burning in every moment
And not the lifetime of one man only
But of old stones that cannot be deciphered.
There is a time for the evening under starlight,
A time for the evening under lamplight
(The evening with the photograph album).
Love is most nearly itself
When here and now cease to matter.
Old men ought to be explorers
Here and there does not matter
We must be still and still moving

Into another intensity
For a further union, a deeper communion
Through the dark cold and the empty desolation,
The wave cry, the wind cry, the vast waters
Of the petrel and the porpoise. In my end is my beginning.

(T.S.Eliot, 1888-1965 *from* `East Coker`, 1940, publ. in Four Quartets, 1944)

NAE REGRETS

I'm growin' auld, still it seems
Life's no jist empty o' its dreams,
In waukrift nichts there comes tae me *wakeful nights*
Memories o' whit used tae be.

retty rough A gey roch road, fell snell weather, *killingly sharp*
ight A fecht tae mak it a wee bit smoother,
Gin we show oor eident grit *stubborn courage*
We'll mak it even better yet.

Langs the road and steys the brae, *steep the hill*
We'll no lament, we've hae'en oor day.
Tho' it wisna' a' it shoulda been,
1 pretty obstinate climb A gey thrawn speil, sma' rests atween.

I'm growin' auld, I feel gey prood,
In youth I ta'en the raugle road, *rough*
Gin I'd my time a'ower again
I'd spend it jist as I hae dune.

(Mary Brooksbank, 1898-1980 [see frontispiece]; Communist leader of unemployed women in Scotland in the 1920s and 30s, *from* Sidlaw Breezes, 1967)

SONNET, CONSOLATION

Do you think now, my friends, that it is time
To look at little things, as long ago
We studied life as children in our prime,
To look at insects, feathers, grass … to watch things grow,

Find tiny treasures, try to enjoy once more
The savoury smells of matches, leaves and stones,
Try to regard the large things as a bore.
Forget the newspapers and telephones,

Reports of agonies where once we dreamed
A springing hope, a glorious time to come.
Nothing is anymore what once it seemed
Evil triumphant beats its bloody drum.

With courage once we strove the world to free,
Now we'll be glad to help one bumble-bee.

(Mary Cowan, 1914- , former health worker for the LCC in Bethnal Green, a Communist from the 1930s, she worked in Vietnam 1975-7 on translations of Vietnamese literature, including an anthology of Vietnamese poetry)

ON SISYPHUS

Unable to roll up that boulder,
that boulder or whatever it was, maybe gneiss,
maybe paper,
I decided the fault lay with me.
The important thing about faults is that they can
be corrected, my mother used to say.

I decided the fault lay with me.
So I added to the boulder
as much weight again. Whatever it was,
maybe hate, maybe love.
And at once it went better. Because

of the certainty that it would
probably break my neck.

Then came the tea-break.
And I realised
that hysteria doesn't solve anything.

(Miroslav Holub, 1923-1998 *from* `On the Contrary`, 1982, transl. from the Czech by Ewald Osers, republished in Poems Before and After, 1990)

THE COALS

Before my mother's hysterectomy
she cried, and told me she must never bring
coals in from the cellar outside the house,
someone must do it for her. The thing itself
I knew was nothing, it was the thought
of that dependence. Her tears shocked me
like a blow. As once she had been taught,
I was taught self-reliance, discipline,
which is both good and bad. You get things done,
you feel you keep the waste and darkness back
by acts and acts and acts and acts and acts,
bridling if someone tells you this is vain,
learning at last in pain. Hardest of all
is to forgive yourself for things undone,
guilt that can poison life – away with it,
you say, and it is loath to go away.
I learned both love and joy in a hard school
and treasure them like the fierce salvage of
some wreck that has been built to look like stone
and stand, though it did not, a thousand years.

(Edwin Morgan 1920 -, *from* Poems of Thirty Years, 1982, republ. in Collected Poems, 2000)

TO MY FRIENDS

Dear friends, and here I say friends
In the broad sense of the word:
Wife, sister, associates, relatives,
Schoolmates of both sexes,
People seen only once
Or frequented all my life;
Provided that between us, for at least a moment,
A line has been stretched,
A well-defined bond.

I speak for you, companions of a crowded
Road, not without its difficulties,
And for you too, who have lost
Soul, courage, the desire to live;
Or no one, or someone, or perhaps
  only one person, or you
Who are reading me: remember the time
Before the wax hardened,
When everyone was like a seal.
Each of us bears the imprint
Of a friend met along the way;
In each the trace of each.
For good or evil
In wisdom or in folly
Everyone stamped by everyone.

Now that time crowds in
And the undertakings are finished,
To all of you the humble wish
That autumn will be long and mild.

(Primo Levi, 1919-1987, transl from the Italian by Ruth Feldman and Brian Swann,
from Friendship, poems ed. by Peter Washington, Everyman, 1995)

RESIDUES

My mother dying left a wardrobeful,
A world half-worn, half-new:
Old-fashioned underclothes; a row of shoes,
Soles upward, staring: tangles of rings,
Impatient opals, bargain bangles, pearls;
And, flowered or jazzy, rayon, cotton, tulle,
A hundred dresses, waiting.

Left with that ragged past,
My poor truncated father sold the lot.
What could he do? The dealer shrugged, and said,
`Take it or leave it- up to you.` He took
And lost the fiver at the races.
The empty wardrobe stared at him for years.

My father dying left a pack of cards,
A presentation clock, a cardboard box
Half-filled with his identity; no books,
No papers. His truncated past
Whisked from my hands, he stepped aside, was gone,
Leaving no litter.

And I, on dying? For my sons, my wife,
My house, my rows of books, my piles of papers,
My mother's letters and my father's clock:
My residue imposing on them all?
Too much, too much.

(Laurence Lerner, 1925 - , from Rembrandt's Mirror, 1987)

`"Let retirement be retirement indeed," he exclaimed, anticipating the changes in the liturgy of the Church`

The pretences are done with.
The eavesdropper at the door
is a fiction. The well-bred

Amens to the formal
Orisons have begun to fade.
I am left with the look

on the sky I need not
try turning into an expression.
Have I been brought here

to repent of my sermons,
to erect silence's stone over
my remains, and to learn

from the lichen's slowness
at work something of the slowness
of the illumination of the self?

(R.S.Thomas, 1913-2000 *from* The Echoes Return Slow, 1988)

STOCKTAKING

Three score achieved, secured with pen and ink:
Prescriptions free and half fare on the train,
The pension pennies trickle from the bank.

Reductions now at concerts make you blink
And study price-lists with new eyes again.
Three score achieved, secured with pen and ink.

What else is cheaper? Neither food nor drink
But haircuts, inch by inch the same refrain:
The pension pennies trickle from the bank.

Where up to now you spurned the truth and sank
Years that appeared too many and a stain:
Three score achieved, secured with pen and ink.

True, waistlines will expand and chests will sink
All despite eating fibres, wholefood grain.
The pension pennies trickle from the bank.

And what of passions, hope, the heartbeat lump
Thudding in throat and voice? All still remain.
Threescore achieved, secured with pen and ink.
The pension pennies trickle from the bank.

(Lotte Kramer, 1923 – *from* The Shoemaker's Wife, 1987)

Surviving

ON HIS BALDNESS

At dawn I sighed to see my hairs fall:
At dusk I sighed to see my hairs fall.
For I dreaded the time when the last lock should go…
They are all gone and I do not mind at all!

(Po Chu-I, [c. 834 A.D.] translated by Arthur Waley)

Four ills, of all my hates the chief,
Are met in me together:
Coughing, old age, sickness, grief…

No girl wants me, no friend haunts me,
Age daunts and enwalls me.
Ah Death, why don't you call me?

(from Anon, 'Hateful Old Age', 9thc. Welsh; translated and reprinted in More Poetry Please!, Everyman, 1997)

---

daily courage doesn't count
we don't get diplomas for it.

ALTA
(Alta Gerrey, from i am not a practicing angel, New York, 1975)

OLD AGE

(Addressed to Liu Yu-hsi, born in the same year)

We are growing old together, you and I;
Let us ask ourselves, what is age like?
The dull eye is closed ere night comes;
The idle head, still uncombed at noon.
Propped on a staff, sometimes a walk abroad;
Or all day sitting with closed doors.
One dares not look in the mirror's polished face;
One cannot read small-letter books.
Deeper and deeper one's love of old friends;
Fewer and fewer, one's dealings with young men.
One thing only, the pleasure of idle talk,
Is as great as ever, when you and I meet.

(Po Chiu-I, A.D.835, translated by Arthur Waley,
More Translations from the Chinese, 1915)

OLD AGE

In the Springtime I am always
Sorry the nights are so short.
My lamp is burning out, the flame
Is low. Flying insects circle
About it. I am sick. My eyes
Are dry and dull. If I sit
Too long in one position,
All my bones ache. Chance thoughts from
I don't know where crowd upon me.
When I get to the end of a
Train of thought, I have forgotten
The beginning. For one thing
I retain I forget ten.
When I was young I liked to read
Now I am too old to make
The effort. Then, too, if I come
Across something interesting
I have no one to talk to
About it. Sad and alone,
I sigh with self pity.

(Ou Yang Hsiu, 1007-1072, transl. by Kenneth Rexroth,
from One Hundred Poems from the Chinese)

SONNET 73

That time of year thou mayst in me behold,
When yellow leaves, or none, or few do hang
Upon those boughs which shake against the cold,
Bare ruined choirs, where late the sweet birds sang.

In me thou see'st the twilight of such day,
As after sunset fadeth in the west,
Which by and by black night doth take away,
Death's second self that seals up all in rest.

In me thou see'st the glowing of such fire
That on the ashes of his youth doth lie,
As the death bed, whereon it must expire,
Consum'd with that which it was nourish'd by.

This thou perceiv'st, which makes thy love more strong,
To love that well, which thou must leave ere long.

(Shakespeare, 1564-1616, first published 1609)

LATER LIFE – SONNET 17

Something this foggy day, a something which
Is neither of this fog nor of today,
Has set me dreaming of the winds that play
Past certain cliffs, along one certain beach,
And turn the topmost edge of waves to spray;
Ah pleasant pebbly strand so far away,
So out of reach while quite within my reach,
As out of reach as India or Cathay!
I am sick of where I am and where I am not,
I am sick of foresight and of memory,
I am sick of all I have and all I see,
I am sick of self, and there is nothing new;
Oh weary impatience of my lot! -
Thus with myself: how fares it, Friends, with you?

(Christina Rossetti, 1830-1894, from Monna Innominata,
[Unnamed Lady] A Sonnet of Sonnets, after 1880)

I LOOK INTO MY GLASS

I look into my glass,
And view my wasting skin,
And say, `Would God it came to pass
My heart had shrunk as thin! `

For then, I, undistrest
By hearts grown cold to me,
Could lonely wait my endless rest
With equanimity.

But Time, to make me grieve,
Part steals, lets part abide;
And shakes this fragile frame at eve
With throbbings of noontide.

(from Wessex Poems, by Thomas Hardy, 1840-1928, written before 1898)

... THE FACE IN THE MIRROR

Gray haunted eyes, absent-mindedly glaring
From wide, uneven orbits; one brow drooping
Somewhat over the eye
Because of a missile fragment still inhering,
Skin deep, as a foolish record of old-world fighting.

Crookedly broken nose – low tackling caused it;
Cheeks, furrowed; coarse gray hair, flying frenetic;
Forehead, wrinkled and high;
Jowls, prominent; ears, large; jaw, pugilistic;
Teeth few; lips, full and ruddy; mouth, ascetic.

I pause with razor poised, scowling derision
At the mirrored man whose beard needs my attention,
And once more ask him why
He still stands ready, with a boy's presumption,
To court the queen in her high silk pavilion.

(Robert Graves, 1895-1985, written c. 1960)

ONE ART

The art of losing isn't hard to master;
so many things seem filled with the intent
to be lost that their loss is no disaster.

Lose something every day. Accept the fluster
of lost door keys, the hour badly spent.
The art of losing isn't hard to master

Then practice losing farther, losing faster:
Places, and names, and where it was you meant
to travel. None of these will bring disaster.

I lost my mother's watch. And look! My last, or
next-to-last, of three loved houses went.
The art of losing isn't hard to master.

I lost two cities, lovely ones. And, vaster,
some realms I owned, two rivers, a continent,
I miss them, but it wasn't a disaster.

- Even losing you (the joking voice, a gesture
I love) I shan't have lied. It's evident
The art of losing's not too hard to master
Though it may look like (*Write* it!) like disaster.

(Elizabeth Bishop, 1911-1979, written c. 1975)

WALKING OUR BOUNDARIES [after surviving cancer]

This first bright day has broken
the back of winter.
We rise from war
to walk across the earth
around our house
both stunned that sun can shine so brightly
after all our pain. …

I take your hand beside the compost heap
glad to be alive and still
with you
we talk of ordinary articles
with relief
while we peer upward
each half-afraid
there will be no tight buds started
on our ancient apple tree
so badly damaged by last winter's storm
knowing
it does not pay to cherish symbols
when the substance
lies so close at hand
waiting to be held

your hand
falls off the apple bark
like casual fire
along my back
my shoulders are dead leaves
waiting to be burned
to life.

The sun is watery warm
our voices
seem too loud for this small yard
too tentative for women
so in love
the siding has come loose in spots
our footsteps hold this place
together
as our place
our joint decisions make the possible
whole.
I do not know when
we shall laugh again
but next week
we will spade up another plot
for this spring's seeding.

(Audre Lorde, 1934-1992, *from* The Black Unicorn, 1978)

A PATIENT OLD CRIPPLE

(from the poem "*Life and Turgid Times of A.Citizen")*

When I am out of sorts with the things
The world is made of, and box lids
Come off with a jerk sideways, scattering
The little things I can't pick up
Screws and buttons, bits of paper, pencils,
I think how I so loved the world once, as did someone else,
And remember hands that are beautiful – In pictures:
Soft and straight; fingers with tender pink nails;
And hips and legs an advantage, not crisis in women.
Then I think
To birds my hands would not be hideous
A useful claw (they would see) not white
And strengthless and slabby and straight – so unprehensile.
The hand of my grandchild and mine are the same thing
As a word said differently is the same at root.
I curse the world that blunders into me, and hurts
But know
Its bad fit is the best that we can do.

(Jenny Joseph, 1932 - *from* Selected Poems, Bloodaxe Books, 1992, reprinted in We Have Come Through, 100 Poems celebrating courage in overcoming depression and trauma, ed. Forbes, Bloodaxe Books, 2003)

TO MY SENSES

Old ears and eyes, so long my patient friends,
For you this silicon nerve and resin lens.
Guides when I heard and saw, yet deaf and blind
Stumbled astray in the mazes of my mind,
Let me assist you now I've lived to see
Far in the dark of what I have to be.

Shunted outside the hubbub of exchange,
Knowledge arrives, articulate and strange,
Voice without breath, light without sun or switch
Beamed from the pulse of an old awareness which
Tells me to age by love and not to cling
To ears, eyes, teeth, knees, hands – or any thing.

(Anne Stevenson 1933 - , *from* The Other House, 1990)

Resisting - not just age

I spit into the face of Time
That has transfigured me.

(W.B.Yeats, 1870-1939, `The Lamentation of the Old Pensioner` [revised ending after 1925])

Did all old men and women rich and poor,
Who trod upon these rocks or passed this door,
Whether in public or in secret rage
As I do now against old age? …

(W.B.Yeats, The Tower, 1926)

`To the Movement women who tell me to stop futzing around with poetry and write plays`

Any one who tells me what to do
Sounds just like anyone else
Who tells me what to do.
ALTA

(Alta Gerrey, *from* I am not a practicing angel, New York, 1975)

NO TRUCE WITH THE FURIES

(R.S.Thomas' title of his last selection of poems, in Collected Later Poems, 1995)

BLAMING SONS

(An apology for his own drunkenness)

White hair covers my temples,
I am wrinkled and gnarled beyond repair,
And though I have got five sons,
They all hate paper and brush.
A-Shu is sixteen;
For laziness there is none like him,
A-hsuian does his best,
But really loathes the Fine Arts.
Yung and Tuan are thirteen,
But do not know `six` from `seven`.
Tung-tzu in his ninth year
Is only concerned with things to eat.
If Heaven treats me like this
What can I do but fill my cup?

(T'ao Ch'ien, 372-427 AD, translated by Arthur Waley)

I AM A UNION WOMAN

I am a union woman,
As brave as I can be
I do not like the bosses,
And the bosses don't like me

Refrain:

Join the NMU
Come join the NMU

I was raised in old Kentucky,
In Kentucky borned and bred;
And when I joined the union
They called me a Rooshian Red.

When my husband asked the boss for a job
These is the words he said:
"Bill Jackson, I can't work you sir,
Your wife's a Rooshian red."

This is the worst time on earth
That I have ever saw;
To get shot down by gun thugs
And framed up by the law.

If you want to join a union
As strong as one can be,
Join the dear old NMU
And come along with me….

The bosses ride fine horses
While we walk in the mud;
Their banner is a dollar sign
While ours is striped with blood.

('Aunt' Molly Jackson, 1880-1961; married at fourteen to a coal miner, she learned to read and write and became a midwife. Mining accidents killed her father, her husband and her son. Blacklisted and forced to leave Kentucky in 1931, she became a singer of protest songs for years after, travelling the USA.)

18 DEMPSTER STREET – THE GUID AULD BAD DAYS

… Jist a wee bit but and half a ben, *one and a half roomed cottage*
When I look back I aye wonder;
Hoo we a' lived I dinna ken
Wi' nine o' us crammed in yonder.

Dinna speak tae me o' the guid auld days,
For wha mair than me kens better;
Wha ran barefitted in ragged claes
In summer days and winter.

Guid days they were for some, nae doot,
But never for me or mine;
Puir, hard-working, aye daein' withoot,
And hungry mony's the time. …

Dae ye mind when we marched roon' and roon',
Sae hopeless and despairing;
The workless outcasts o' this toon,
Few cared hoo we were farin'.

Full twenty thousand unemployed,
W' their wives and bits o' bairns;
And whit was the staple diet enjoyed,
Breid and marge wi' a puckle ham pairin's. … *a few bacon rin*

Ye'll mind o' the days,for they're no sae auld,
When ye rose aboot five in the morning
Tae cairry yer bairnies oot in the cauld,
A gey puir livin' then we were earning. …

Now you dear ladies, awa' hame tae yer men,
Coont your blessings, thank God and yer neighbour
For a' we've been through, gin you've brains ye should ken,
You were lucky we jist voted Labour.

(Mary Brooksbank, [see frontispiece] 1896-1980, mill-worker from the age of eleven, Communist leader of unemployed women in Dundee in the 1920s. Imprisoned for `obstructing` mounted police charges, she started to write poetry and songs for her violin and would go and perform in old folks' clubs to the last. *From* Sidlaw Breezes, 1967)

from POEM

I lived in the first century of the world wars.
Most mornings I would be more or less insane,
The newspapers would arrive with their careless stories,
The news would pour out of various devices
Interrupted by attempts to sell products to the unseen.
I would call my friends on other devices;
They would be more or less mad for similar reasons….
I lived in the first century of these wars.

(Muriel Rukeyser, 1913-1982 lifelong war resister, was arrested and briefly imprisoned for her public protests against the Vietnam War, 1973. *From* 'The Speed of Darkness', 1968)

---

from LOOKING

Battles whose names I do not know
Weapons whose wish they dare not teach
Wars whose need they will not show
Tear us tear us each from each, …

(Muriel Rukeyser, 1913-1978, *from* 'Breaking Open', 1973)

---

from WHEREVER

… Wherever
We protest
We will go planting

Make poems
Seed grass
Feed a child growing
Build a house
Whatever we stand against
We will stand feeding and seeding …

(Muriel Rukeyser, 1913-1982, *from* 'Breaking Open', 1973)

DIRGE WITHOUT MUSIC

I am not resigned to the shutting away of loving hearts in the hard ground.
So it is, and so it will be, for so it has been, time out of mind:
Into the darkness they go, the wise and the lovely. Crowned
With lilies and with laurel they go; but I am not resigned.

Lovers and thinkers, into the earth with you.
Be one with the dull, the indiscriminate dust.
A fragment of what you felt, of what you knew,
A formula, a phrase remains, - but the best is lost.

The answers quick and keen, the honest look, the laughter, the love, -
They are gone. They are gone to feed the roses. Elegant and curled
Is the blossom. Fragrant is the blossom. I know. But I do not approve.
More precious was the light in your eyes than all the roses in the world.

Down, down, down into the darkness of the grave
Gently they go, the beautiful, the tender, the kind;
Gently they go, the intelligent, the witty, the brave
I know. But I do not approve. And I am not resigned.

(Edna St. Vincent Millay 1892-1950)

`DO NOT GO GENTLE INTO THAT GOOD NIGHT`

Do not go gentle into that good night,
Old age should burn and rave at close of day;
Rage, rage against the dying of the light.

Though wise men at their end know dark is right,
Because their words had forked no lightning they
Do not go gentle into that good night.

Good men, the last wave by, crying how bright
Their frail deeds might have danced in a green bay,
Rage, rage against the dying of the light.

Wild men who caught and sang the sun in flight,
And learn, too late, they grieved it on its way,
Do not go gentle into that good night.

Grave men, near death, who see with blinding sight
Blind eyes could blaze like meteors and be gay,
Rage, rage against the dying of the light.

And you, my father, there on the sad height,
Curse, bless, me now with your fierce tears, I pray.
Do not go gentle into that goodnight.
Rage, rage against the dying of the light.

(Dylan Thomas 1914-1953, written 1952)

A REPLY TO DYLAN THOMAS

Why not go gentle into that good night?
One knows the night is good so why rebel
When strength is squandered in a hopeless fight?

Of course it's hopeless: it is mankind's plight
And since for all is tolled the passing bell
Why not go gentle into that good night

Forever free of calumny and spite?
It makes no sense to rage against the knell
When strength is squandered in a hopeless fight. ...

(D. Shepherd, first prize winner in Literary Review Poetry Competition, `Night and Day`, June 2006)

COURAGE

I will not be the slave to any love.
To no one
will I hand over my purpose in life,
my right to go on growing
to my very last breath.

Fettered by the dark instinct of motherhood,
gasping for love like an asthmatic for air,
it's such an effort to build in myself
my beautiful human egoism,
reserved for centuries
for men.

Against me
are all the civilisations of the world,
all the holy books of mankind,
written in a flash of lightning
by the eloquent pens of mystic angels.
Ten Mohammeds
in ten stylishly mouldy languages
threaten me with damnation
on earth and in eternal heaven.

Against me
is my own heart.
Trained for millennia
in the inhuman virtue of sacrifice.

(Anna Swir 1909-1984, *from* Fat Like The Sun, transl. from the
Polish by Margaret Marshment and Grazyna Baran, 1986)

Lying Awake At Night

I wake and feel the fell of dark, not day ...

My own heart let me more have pity on; let
Me live to my sad self hereafter kind,
Charitable; not live this tormented mind
With this tormented mind tormenting yet ...
Leave comfort root-room ...

(Gerard Manley Hopkins, 1844-1889, Sonnets)

If I were asked: `What is now the chief and fundamental
fact of your existence? ` I would reply: `Insomnia`.

(Anton Chekhov, A Boring Story, From an Old Man's Notebook, 1889)

NIGHT THOUGHTS

I cannot sleep. The long, long
Night is full of bitterness.
I sit alone in my room,
Beside a smoky lamp.
I rub my heavy eyelids
And idly turn the pages
Of my book. Again and again
I trim my brush and stir the ink.
The hours go by. The moon comes
In the open window, pale
And bright like new money.
At last I fall asleep and
I dream of the days on the
River at Tsa-feng, and the
Friends of my youth in Yen Chao.
Young and happy we ran
Over the beautiful hills.
And now the years have gone by,
And I have never gone back.

(Liu Yu-Hsi, 1125-1209 transl. by Kenneth Rexroth, in One Hundred Poems from the Chinese)

ALONE IN THE NIGHT
[written after the death of her husband]

The warm rain and pure wind
Have just freed the willows from
The ice. As I watch the peach trees,
Spring rises from my heart and blooms on
My cheeks. My mind is unsteady,
As if I were drunk. I try
To write a poem in which
My tears will flow together
With your tears. My rouge is stale.
My hairpins are too heavy.
I throw myself across my
Gold cushions, wrapped in my lonely
Doubled quilt, and crush the phoenixes
In my headdress. Alone, deep
In bitter loneliness, without
Even a good dream, I lie,
Trimming the lamp in the passing night.

(Li Ch'ing Chao, 1081-1140, China's greatest poetess according to the translator Kenneth Rexroth *from* One Hundred Poems from the Chinese)

Does the imagination dwell the most
Upon a woman won or woman lost?
If on the lost, admit you turned aside
From a great labyrinth out of pride,
Cowardice, some silly over-subtle thought
Or anything called conscience once;
And that if memory recur, the sun's
Under eclipse and the day blotted out. …

(Yeats, 1865-1939, *from* `The Tower`, 1926)

…Although the summer sunlight gild
Cloudy leafage of the sky,
Or wintry moonlight sink the field
In storm-scattered intricacy,
I cannot look thereon,
Responsibility so weighs me down.

Things said or done long years ago,
Or things I did not do or say
But thought that I might say or do,
Weigh me down, and not a day
But something is recalled,
My conscience or my vanity appalled.

(Yeats, 1865-1939, `Vacillation` *from* The Winding Stair, 1933)

…All that I have said and done,
Now that I am old and ill,
Turns into a question till
I lie awake night after night
And never get the answers right.
Did that play of mine send out
Certain men the English shot?
Did words of mine put too great strain
On that woman's reeling brain?
Could my spoken words have checked
That whereby a house lay wrecked?
And all seems evil until I
Sleepless would lie down and die …

(Yeats, 1865-1939, `The Man and the Echo` *from* Last Poems, 1936-1939)

... Let me disclose the gifts reserved for age
To set a crown upon your lifetime's effort.
First, the cold friction of expiring sense
Without enchantment, offering no promise
But bitter tastelessness of shadow fruit
As body and soul begin to fall asunder.
Second, the conscious impotence of rage
At human folly, and the laceration
Of laughter at what ceases to amuse.
And last, the rending pain of re-enactment
Of all that you have done, and been; the shame
Of motives late revealed, and the awareness
Of things ill done and done to others' harm
Which once you took for exercise of virtue. ...

(T.S.Eliot, 1886-1965, from `Little Gidding`, 1942, in Four Quartets, 1944)

AUBADE

I work all day, and get half-drunk at night.
Waking at four to soundless dark, I stare.
In time the curtain-edges will grow light.
Till then I see what's really always there:
Unresting death, a whole day nearer now,
Making all thought impossible but how
And where and when I shall myself die.
Arid interrogation: yet the dread
Of dying, and being dead,
Flashes afresh to hold and horrify.

The mind blanks at the glare. Not in remorse
-The good not done, the love not given, time
Torn off unused – nor wretchedly because
An only life can take so long to climb
Clear of its wrong beginnings, and may never;
But at the total emptiness for ever,
The sure extinction that we travel to
And shall be lost in always. Not to be here,
Not to be anywhere,
And soon; nothing more terrible, nothing more true.

This is a special way of being afraid
No trick dispels. Religion used to try,
That vast moth-eaten musical brocade
Created to pretend we never die,
And specious stuff that says *No rational being*
Can fear a thing it will not feel, not seeing
That this is what we fear – no sight, no sound,
No touch or taste or smell, nothing to think with,
Nothing to love or link with,
The anaesthetic from which none come round.

And so it stays just on the edge of vision,
A small unfocused blur, a standing chill
That slows each impulse down to indecision.
Most things may never happen: this one will,
And realisation of it rages out
In furnace-fear when we are caught without
People or drink. Courage is no good:
It means not scaring others. Being brave
Lets no one off the grave.
Death is no different whined at than withstood.

Slowly light strengthens, and the room takes shape.
It stands plain as a wardrobe, what we know,
Have always known, know that we can't escape,
Yet can't accept. One side will have to go.
Meanwhile telephones crouch getting ready to ring
In locked-up offices, and all the uncaring
Intricate rented world begins to rouse.
The sky is white as clay, with no sun.
Work has to be done.
Postmen like doctors go from house to house.

(Philip Larkin, 1922-1985, 29 Nov. 1977)

THINGS

There are worse things than having behaved foolishly in public.
There are worse things than these miniature betrayals
committed or endured or suspected; there are worse things
than not being able to sleep for thinking about them.
It is 5 a.m. All the worse things come stalking in
and stand icily about the bed looking worse and worse and worse.

(Fleur Adcock, 1934 - , publ. 1979)

HE RESIGNS

Age, and the deaths, and the ghosts.
Her having gone away
in spirit from me. Hosts
of regrets come and find me empty.

I don't feel this will change.
I don't want any thing
or person, familiar or strange.
I don't think I will sing

any more just now;
ever. I must start
to sit with a blind brow
above an empty heart.

(John Berryman, 1914-1972; last poem)

Seeing the Funny Side

When the cottage chimney smokes,
And wanton greybeards crack their jokes
By the glowing ember's light, …

(Thomas Holcroft, `The Seasons` c.1793)

`[The] doubtful honour of a brief transit through a sorry world hardly [calls] for effusiveness` …

(Thomas Hardy, last paragraph of The Mayor of Casterbridge, 1886)

`Humour – the only faculty that improves with age`.

(Ethel Smyth)

`… there will be humour,
for that is the final guest to leave
the human house'….

(Kit Wright, `Advice for Attending a Hundredth Birthday Party`, *from* Hoping It Might Be So, 2000)

The Last Laugh

I made hay while the sun shone.
My work sold.
Now, if the harvest is over
And the world cold,
Give me the bonus of laughter
As I lose hold.

(John Betjeman, A Nip in the Air, 1974)

DRINKING WITH FRIENDS
AMONGST THE BLOOMING PEONIES

We had a drinking party
To admire the peonies.
I drank cup after cup till
I was drunk. Then to my shame
I heard the flowers whisper.
"What are we doing, blooming
For these old alcoholics?"

(Liu Yu-Hsi 772-842, from Love and the TurningYear – 100 More Poems from the Chinese, by Kenneth Rexroth)

GET UP AND BAR THE DOOR

There leeved a wee man at the fit of yon hill
  John Blunt it was his name, O
And he selld liquor and ale the best,
  And bears a wondrous fame, O
Tal lara ta lilt, tal lara a lilt
Tal lara ta lilt, tal lara.

The win it blew frae north to south
  It blew into the floor;
Says auld John Blunt to Janet the wife,
"Ye maun rise up and bar the door."

"My hans are in my hussyskep,
  I canna weel get them free,
And if ye dinnar bar it yersel
  It'll never be barred by me."

They made it up atween them twa,
  They made it unco sure,
That the ane that spoke the foremost word
  Was to rise and bar the door.

There was twa travellers travelling late,
  Was travelling cross the muir,
And they cam unto wee John Blunt's,
  Just by the light o the door.

"O whether is this a rich man's house,
  Or whether is it a puir?"
But never a word would the auld bodies speak,
  For the barring o the door.

First they bad good een to them,
  And syne they bad good morrow;
But never a word would the auld bodies speak,
  For the barring o the door, O.

First they ate the white puddin,
  And syne they ate the black,
And aye the auld wife said to herself,
  May the deil slip doun wi that!

And next they drank o the liquor sae strong,
  And syne they drank o the yill:
"Now since we hae got a house o our ain
  I'm sure we may tak our fill."

It's says, the ane unto the ither,
  "Here, man, tak ye my knife,
An ye'll scrape aff the auld man's beard,
  While I kiss the gudewife."

"Ye hae eaten my meat, ye hae drucken my drink,
  Ye'd make my auld wife a whore!"
"John Blunt, ye hae spoken the foremost word,
  Ye maun rise up and bar the door."

(Anon. Scottish ballad; first publ. version, 1769)

VERSES ON THE DEATH OF DR. SWIFT WRITTEN BY HIMSELF: NOV. 1731

The time is not remote, when I
Must by the course of nature die;
When, I foresee, my special friends
Will try to find their private ends:
And though 'tis hardly understood
Which way my death can do them good,
Yet thus, methinks, I hear them speak:
`See, how the Dean begins to break!
`Poor gentleman, he droops apace!
`You plainly find it in his face.
`That old vertigo in his head
`Will never leave him, till he's dead.
`Besides, his memory decays:
`He recollects not what he says;
`He cannot call his friends to mind;
`Forgets the place where last he din'd;
`Plies you with stories o'er and o'er;
`He told them fifty times before.
`How does he fancy we can sit
`To hear his out-of-fashion wit?
`But he takes up with younger folks,
`Who for his wine will bear his jokes.
`Faith! He must make his stories shorter,
`Or change his comrades once a quarter:
`In half the time he talks them round,
`There must another set be found.
`For poetry, he's past his prime:
`He takes an hour to find a rhyme;
`His fire is out, his wit decay'd,
`His fancy sunk, his Muse a jade.
`I'd have him throw away his pen; -
`But there's no talking to some men!`
And then their tenderness appears
By adding largely to my years:
`He's older than he would be reckon'd.
`And well remembers *Charles* the Second.
`He hardly drinks a pint of wine;
`And that I doubt, is no good sign.
`His stomach too begins to fail:

`Last year we thought him strong and hale:
`But now he's quite another thing:
`I wish he may hold out till spring!`
They hug themselves, and reason thus:
`It is not yet so bad with us!`
In such a cases, they talk in tropes,
And by their fears express their hopes.
Some great misfortune to portend,
No enemy can match a friend.
With all the kindness they profess,
The merit of a lucky guess
(When daily *Howd'y's* come of course!
And servants answer `Worse and worse!`)
Would please them better, than to tell
That, `God be prais'd the Dean is well.`
Then he, who prophesied the best,
Approves his foresight to the rest:
`You know I always fear'd the worst,
`And often told you so at first.`
He'd rather choose that I should die,
Than his predictions prove a lie.
Not one foretells I shall recover;
But all agree to give me over.

……………………………………..

Behold the fatal day arrive!
`How is the Dean?` - `He's just alive.`
Now the departing prayer is read;
`He hardly breathes` - `The Dean is dead.`
Before the passing-bell begun,
The news through half the town is run.
`O! may we all for death prepare!
`What has he left? And who's his heir?
`I know no more than what the news is:
`'Tis all bequeath'd to publick uses.
To publick uses! There's a whim!
`What had the publick done for him? …

Why do we grieve that friends should die?
No loss more easy to supply.
One year is past; a different scene!
No farther mention of the Dean;
Who now, alas, no more is miss'd,.
Than if he never did exist. …

(Jonathan Swift 1667-1745)

PORTRAIT OF THE ARTIST AS A PREMATURELY OLD MAN

It is common knowledge to every schoolboy and even every Bachelor of Arts,
That all sin is divided into two parts.
One kind of sin is called a sin of commission, and that is very important,
And it is what you are doing when you are doing something you ortant,
And the other kind of sin is just the opposite and is called a sin of
omission and is equally bad in the eyes of all right-thinking people,
from Billy Sunday to Buddha,
And it consists of not having done something you shuddha.
I might as well give you my opinion of these two kinds of sin as long as,
In a way, against each other we are pitting them,
And that is, don't bother your head about the sins of commission because
however sinful, they must at least be fun or else you wouldn't be
committing them.
It is the sin of omission, the second kind of sin,
That lays eggs under your skin.
The way you get really painfully bitten
Is by the insurance you haven't taken out and the checks you haven't
added up the stubs of and the appointments you haven't kept and
the bills you haven't paid and the letters you haven't written.
Also, about sins of omission there is one particularly painful lack of beauty,
Namely, it isn't as though it had been a riotous red-letter day or night
every time you neglected to do your duty;
You didn't get a wicked forbidden thrill
Every time you let a policy lapse or forgot to pay a bill;
You didn't slap the lads in the tavern on the back and loudly cry Whee,
Let's all fail to write just one more letter before we go home, and this
round of unwritten letters is on me.

No, you never get any fun
Out of the things you haven't done,
But they are the things that I do not like to be amid,
Because the suitable things you didn't do give you a lot more trouble than the unsuitable things you did.
The moral is that it is probably better not to sin at all, but if some kind of sin you must be pursuing,
Well, remember to do it by doing rather than by not doing.

(Ogden Nash 1902-1971)

ANCIENT MUSIC

Winter is icummen in,
Llude sing Goddamm,
Raineth drop and staineth slop,
And how the wind doth ramm!
                Sing: Goddamm.
Skiddeth bus and sloppeth us,
An ague hath my ham.
Freezeth river, turneth liver,
                Damn you, sing: Goddam.
Goddam, Goddamm, 'tis why I am, Goddam,
                So 'gainst the winter's balm.
Sing goddamm, damm, sing Goddamm,
Sing goddamm, sing goddamm, DAMM.

(Ezra Pound, 1885-1972)

GOING TO THE DOGS

My granddad, viewing earth's worn cogs,
Said things were going to the dogs;
His granddad in his house of logs,
Said things were going to the dogs;
His granddad in the Flemish bogs,
Said things were going to the dogs;
His granddad in his old skin togs,
Said things were going to the dogs;
There's one thing that I have to state -
The dogs have had a good long wait.

(Anon. publ. in Wendy Cope, ed. The Funny Side, 101 Humorous Poems, 1998)

MR AND MRS R AND THE CHRISTMAS CARD LIST

Shall I cross them off?
It's twenty years since we last met.

Of course Mr R and I once thought
we were made for each other –

Ah, that heart-stopping moment
by the kitchen sink, when he took off

his spectacles and fiercely kissed me.
But all that lasted less than a week

And what I recall more vividly
is Mrs R's good advice:

Always plunge your lemons in hot water
before you squeeze them.

One more year perhaps.

(Connie Bensley, 1929 -, from Choosing to be a Swan, 1994)

FESTSCHRIFT

Dear So-and-so, you're seventy. Well done!
Or is it sixty? It's a bit confusing
remembering which, of all my ageing friends,
is the one about whose talents I'm enthusing.

I'm getting on myself, a fact which makes one
occasionally vague –as you may know,
having achieved such venerable status;
although in you, of course, the years don't show.

Anyway, I'm delighted to contribute
to the memorial volume which your wife –
or publisher – is secretly arranging
to mark this splendid milestone in your life.

As one of your most passionate admirers
I'm glad to tell the world of my conviction
that you've transformed the course of literature
by your poetry – or do I mean your fiction?

Oh dear. Well, never mind. Congratulations,
from a near contemporary, on your weighty
achievements; and you'll hear this all again
in ten years' time, at seventy – sorry! eighty.

(Fleur Adcock, 1934 -, publ. 1997)

LONG-LEGGED ALLURE

Do those legs belong to me?

Large thick extremities,
Getting ready for the cemetery
Surfaced like ripples on the sea.
Scant, limp hair
Barely there,
Brown patches
Swathe scaling pins
Over superfluous fluted skin.

To whom
Do those legs belong?

Mine, to my memory,
Are sun-kissed,
Tanned and strong,
Pleasing every eye along
Life's pleasurable path.
These days, I look down,
I gasp;
Suppressing the urge to laugh
I ask:
Are those `My` Legs?`

(Diana Ward-Davis, 1940 - , written 2005, included in Brighton and Hove `Celebrating Age` Festival film Street Elders, 2006)

<u>Seizing the Moment</u>

Ah, my soul, seek not after immortal life, but exhaust the fullness of the present.

(Pindar)

When I dance, I dance; and when I sleepe, I sleepe. And when I am solitarie walking in a faire orchard, if my thoughts have a while entertained themselves with strange occurrences, I doe another while bring them to walke with mee in the orchard … What egregious fooles are we? Hee hath past his life in idlenesse, say we; alas! I have done nothing this day. What? have you not lived?…

(Florio's translation of Montaigne's (last) essay, `<u>Of Experience</u>`, 1603)

They are not long, the days of wine and roses:
Out of a misty dream
Our path emerges for a while, then closes
Within a dream.

(Ernest Dowson, 1867-1900)

… Look thy last on all things lovely
Every hour. Let no night
Seal thy sense in deathly slumber
Till to delight
Thou have paid thy utmost blessing;
Since that all things thou wouldst praise
Beauty took from those who loved them
In other days.

(Walter de la Mare, 1873-1956, `Fare Well` c. 1916)

Now I'm an old woman,
So I want the last word:
There is no such thing as time –
Only this very minute
And I'm in it.
Thank the Lord.

(Joyce Grenfell, `Time` from <u>Turn Back the Clock</u>, 1983)

FIVE POEMS ON RETURNING TO LIVE IN THE COUNTRY

No. 5

Downcast and dejected I go home with my staff alone,
On the hazelled path that winds through the mountain coigns.
The torrents of these hills are pure and shallow,
And in their water I may wash my feet.
I filter the wine that I've just heated up,
Then cook a chicken and invite my neighbours in.
As the sun goes down the room is filled with shadows,
So thornwood torches take the place of candles,
Amid such joy I regret the night's so short,
And once again another day is dawning.

(T'ao Ch'ien, 365-427, transl. by J.D.Frodsham in
An Anthology of Chinese Verse, Oxford, Clarendon Press, 1967)

A POND IN A JARDINIERE

1.
Old men are like little boys:
I draw water, fill the jardinière to make a tiny pond.
All night green frogs gabble till dawn,
just like the time I went fishing at Fang-k'ou.

2.
My ceramic lake in dawn, water settled clear,
numberless tiny bugs –I don't know what you call them;
suddenly they dart and scatter, not a shadow left;
only a squadron of baby fish advancing.

3.
Pond shine and sky glow, blue matching blue;
a few bucketfuls of water poured is all that laps these shores.
I'll wait until the night is cold, the bright moon set,
then count how many stars come swimming here.

(Han Yu , 768-824 AD, in Burton Watson, The Columbian
Book of Chinese Poetry from early times to the 13th century)

SOME HOURS THAT ESCAPE FROM TIME

There are some hours that escape from Time;
They are so very still, so very deep:
In a world of dreams they are like dreamless sleep,
In a world of voices they are silences.
I knew one … having lost the old sublime
Adventures that were my youth's mysteries …
I sat still, radiant with a hushed content,
Taking this elder venture for my own,
While the unmeasured moments came and went,
Watching and being watched, knowing and being known.

(Margaret Cropper, 1865? – 195?, written in 1929, in Collected Poems, 1958)

TIME

`Established` is a good word, much used in garden books,
Oh, become established quickly, quickly, garden!
For I am fugitive, I am very fugitive –

Those that come after me will gather these roses,
And watch, as I do now, the white wistaria
Burst, in the sunshine, from its pale green sheathe.

Planned. Planted. Established. Then neglected,
Till at last the loiterer by the gate will wonder
At the old, old cottage, the old wooden cottage,
And say, `One might build here, the view is glorious;
This must have been a pretty garden once.`

(Ursula Bethell 1874-1945, written c. 1929)

THE SILENCE NOW

These days the silence is immense.
It is there deep down, not to be escaped.
The twittering flight of goldfinches,
The three crows cawing in the distance
Only brush the surface of this silence
Full of mourning, the long drawn-out
Tug and sigh of waters never still-
The ocean out there, and the inner ocean.

Only animals comfort because they live
In the present and cannot drag us down
Into those caverns of memory full of loss.
They pay no attention to the thunder
Of distant waves. My dog's eager eyes
Watch me as I sit by the window, thinking.

At the bottom of the silence what lies in wait?
Is it love? Is it death? Too early or too late?
What is it I can have that I still want?

My swift response is to what cannot stay,
The dying daffodils, peonies on the way.
Iris just opening, lilac turning brown
In the immense silence where I live alone.

It is the transient that touches me, old,
Those light-shot clouds as the sky clears,
A passing glory can still move to tears,
Moments of pure joy like some fairy gold
Too evanescent to be kept or told.
And the cat's soft footfall on the stair
Keeps me alive, makes Nowhere into Here.
At the bottom of the silence it is she
Who speaks of an eternal Now to me.

(May Sarton 1912-1995, written when she was 76)

THE HAPPY THREE

Inside, my darling wife
Sharpened a butcher knife;
Sighed out her pure relief
  That I was gone.

When I had tried to clean
My papers up, between
Words skirting the obscene
  She frowned her frown.

Shelves have a special use;
And Why muddy shoes
In with your underclothes?
  She asked, woman.

So I betook myself
With not one tiny laugh
To drink some half-and-half
  On the back lawn.

Who should come up right then,
But our goose, Marianne,
Having escaped her pen,
  Hunting the sun.

Named for a poetess,
(Whom I like none-the-less)
Her pure-white featheriness
  She paused to preen;

But when she pecked my toe,
My banked-up vertigo
Vanished like April snow;
  All rage was gone.

Then a close towhee, a
Phoebe not far away
Sang out audaciously
  Notes finely drawn.

Back to the house we ran,
Me, and dear Marianne –
Then we romped out again,
  Out again,
  Out again,
  Three in the sun.

(Theodore Roethke, 1908-1963, Selected Poems, 1969)

GETTING OLDER

The first surprise: I like it.
Whatever happens now, some things
that used to terrify have not.

I didn't die young, for instance. Or lose
my only love. My three children
never had to run away from anyone.

Don't tell me this gratitude is complacent.
We all approach the edge of the same blackness
which for me is silent.

Knowing as much sharpens
my delight in January freesia,
hot coffee, winter sunlight. So we say

as we lie close on some gentle occasion:
every day won from such
darkness is a celebration.

(Elaine Feinstein 1930 -)

Having faith

Yea though I walk through the valley of the shadow of death, I will fear no evil: for thou art with me, thy rod and staff they comfort me.

(23rd Psalm)

`Lord now lettest thou thy servant depart in peace,
according to thy word.
For mine eyes have seen thy salvation.`

(The aged Simeon's words, quoted in Luke, chapter 2, verses 29-30, and used as *Nunc Dimittis* at Evensong in The Book of Common Prayer)

What are these which are arrayed in white robes? And whence came they?...
And he said to me `These are they which came out of great tribulation ...
They shall hunger no more, neither thirst any more; neither shall the sun light on them nor any heat.
... and God shall wipe away all tears from their eyes.`

(Book of Revelation, ch. 7, verses 13-17)

Jerusalem the golden,
With milk and honey blest
Beneath thy contemplation
Sink heart and voice opprest.
I know not, Oh, I know not
What joys await us there,
What radiancy of glory,
What bliss beyond compare....

(Bernard of Cluny, 12th C. `Urbs Sion aurea`)

The day thou gavest Lord is ended
The darkness falls at thy behest ...

(Hymns Ancient and Modern)

HIERUSALEM

Hierusalem, my happy home,
When shall I come to thee?
When shall my sorrows have an end,
Thy joys when shall I see?

O happy harbour of the saints,
O sweet and pleasant soil,
In thee no sorrow may be found,
No grief, no care, no toil.

There lust and lucre cannot dwell,
There envy bears no sway;
There is no hunger, heat, nor cold,
But pleasure every way. …

Ah, my sweet home, Hierusalem,
Would God I were in thee!
Would God my woes were at an end,
The joys that I might see!

Thy gardens and thy gallant walks
Continually are green;
There grows such sweet and pleasant flowers
As nowhere else are seen.

Quite through the streets, with silver sound,
The flood of life doth flow;
Upon whose banks on every side
The wood of life doth grow.

Our Lady sings *Magnificat*
With tune surpassing sweet,
And all the virgins bear their part
Sitting about her feet.

Hierusalem, my happy home,
Would God I were in thee!
Would God my woes were at an end,
The joys that I might see!

(Anon, early 16th Century)

THE PRAIS OF AIGE

Wythin a garth, under a red rosere,
Ane ald man, and decrepit, herd I syng;
Gay was the note, suete was the voce et clere;
It was grete joy to here of sik a thing.
`And to my dome,` he said in his dytyng,
`For to be young I wald not, for my wis
Off all this warld to make me lord et king;
The more of age the nerar hevynnis blis. …

(Robert Henryson, c.1425-c.1508)

NEVER WEATHER-BEATEN SAILE

Never weather-beaten Saile more willing bent to shore,
Never tyred Pilgrim's limbs affected slumber more;
Then my weary spright now longs to flye out of my troubled brest.
O come quickly, sweetest Lord, and take my soule to rest!

Ever blooming are the joyes of Heav'n's high paradise,
Cold age deafes not there our eares nor vapour dims our eyes:
Glory there the sun outshines, whose beames the blessed onely see.
O come quickly, glorious Lord, and raise my spright to thee!

(Thomas Campion, 1567-1620, from Book of Ayres, c.1613)

HYMNE TO GOD MY GOD, IN MY SICKNESSE

Since I am coming to that Holy roome,
  Where, with thy Quire of Saints for evermore,
I shall be made thy Musique; As I come
  I tune the Instrument here at the dore,
And what I must doe then, thinke here before.

Whilst my Physitians by their love are growne
  Cosmographers, and I their Mapp, who lie
Flat on this bed, that by them may be showne
  That this is my South-west discoverie
Per fretum febris, by these streights to die,

I joy, that in these straits, I see my West;
  For, though theire currents yeeld returne to none,
What shall my West hurt me? As West and East
  In all flat Maps (and I am one) are one,
So death doth touch the Resurrection....

(John Donne, 1572-1631, written 1623)

---

from THE EXEQUY

Sleep on my *Love* in thy quiet bed
Never to be disquieted!
My last good night! Thou wilt not wake
Till I thy fate shall overtake:
Till age, or grief, or sickness, must
Marry my body to that dust
It so much loves…
Stay for me there; I will not faile
To meet thee in that hollow Vale.
And think not much of my delay;
I am already on the way,
And follow thee with all the speed
Desire can make, or sorrows breed,
Each minute is a short degree,
And ev'ry houre a step towards thee….

But heark, my pulse like a soft drum
Beats my approach, tells *Thee* I come;
And slow howe'er my approaches be,
I shall at last lie down by *Thee*.

The thought of this bids me go on,
And wait my dissolution
With hope and comfort. *Dear* (forgive
The crime) I am content to live
Divided, with but half a heart,
Till we shall meet and never part.

(Henry King, 1592-1669, written on the death of his wife, 1657)

JOY AND PEACE IN BELIEVING

Sometimes a light surprises
 The Christian while he sings;
It is the LORD who rises
 With healing in his wings:
When comforts are declining,
 He grants the soul again
A season of clear shining
 To cheer it after rain. …

(William Cowper, 1731-1800, *from* Olney Hymns, 1779)

AMAZING GRACE

Amazing grace (how sweet the sound)
 That saved a wretch like me.
I once was lost, but now am found,
 Was blind, but now I see.

`Twas grace that taught my heart to fear,
 And grace my fears relieved.
How precious did that grace appear
 The hour I first believed.

Through many dangers, toils and snares,
 I have already come;
`Tis grace hath brought me safe thus far,
 And grace will lead me home.

(John Newton, 1726-1806, converted former slave-trader, *from* Olney Hymns, 1779)

Hush, hush, somebody's calling my name.
Oh my Lord, Lordy, what shall I do?

I'm so glad I got my freedom in time –
Hush, hush, somebody's calling my name.

I'm packing up and getting ready to go
I'm packing up and getting ready to go.
I want to get my freedom over there,
I'm just packing up, I'm getting ready to go.

I want to meet my mother over there
I want to meet my mother over there
I'm just packing up, I'm getting ready to go.

Bye and bye, bye and bye, I'm going to lay down my heavy load.
Oh when I get to heaven I'm going to sing and shout
And nobody there's goin' to turn me out.
Bye and bye, bye and bye, I'm goin' to lay down my heavy load.

Swing low, sweet chariot,
Coming for to carry me home
Swing low, sweet chariot,
Coming for to carry me home.

I looked over Jordan,
And what did I see
Coming for to carry me home?
A band of angels coming after me,
Coming for to carry me home.

ABIDE WITH ME

Abide with me; fast falls the eventide;
The darkness deepens; Lord, with me abide:
When other helpers fail, and comforts flee,
Help of the helpless, O abide with me.

Swift to its close ebbs out life's little day;
Earth's joys grow dim, its glories pass away;
Change and decay in all around I see;
O Thou Who changest not, abide with me....

I fear no foe with Thee at hand to bless;
Ills have no weight, and tears no bitterness;
Where is death's sting? Where, grave, thy victory?
I triumph still, if Thou abide with me.

Hold Thou Thy cross before my closing eyes;
Shine through the gloom, and point me to the skies;
Heav'ns morning breaks, and earth's vain shadows flee;
In life, in death, O Lord, abide with me.

(Henry Francis Lyte, 1793-1847)

---

from IN MEMORIAM

XLIX

Be near me when my light is low,
When the blood creeps, and the nerves prick
And tingle; and the heart is sick,
And all the wheels of Being slow.

Be near me when the sensuous frame
Is racked with pangs that conquer trust;
And Time, a maniac scattering dust,
And Life, a Fury slinging flame. …

Be near me when I fade away,
To point the term of human strife,
And on the low dark verge of life
The twilight of eternal day.

(Tennyson, 1809-1892)

I SHALL KNOW WHY

I shall know why, when time is over,
And I have ceased to wonder why;
Christ will explain each separate anguish
In the fair schoolroom of the sky.

He will tell me what Peter promised,
And I for wonder at his woe,
I shall forget the drop of anguish
That scalds me now, that scalds me now.

(Emily Dickinson, 1830-1886)

THE SHIP OF DEATH

1

Now it is autumn and the falling fruit
and the long journey towards oblivion.

The apples falling like great drops of dew
to bruise themselves an exit from themselves.

And it is time to go, to bid farewell
to one's own self, and find an exit
from the fallen self. ...

7

We are dying, we are dying, so all we can do
is now to be willing to die, and to build the ship
of death to carry the soul on the longest journey.

A little ship, with oars and food
and little dishes, and all accoutrements
fitting and ready for the departing soul.

Now launch the small ship, now as the body dies
and life departs, launch out, the fragile soul
in the fragile ship of courage, the ark of faith
with its store of food and little cooking pans
and change of clothes,
upon the flood's black waste
upon the waters of the end
upon the sea of death, where still we sail
darkly, for we cannot steer and have no port. ...

(D.H.Lawrence, 1885-1930, from Last Poems, 1929)

---

from LITTLE GIDDING

V

What we call the beginning is often the end
And to make an end is to make a beginning.
The end is where we start from....
So, while the light fails
On a winter's afternoon, in a secluded chapel
History is now and England.

With the drawing of this Love and the voice of this Calling

We shall not cease from exploration
And the end of our exploring
Will be to arrive where we started
And know the place for the first time.
Through the unknown, remembered gate
When the last of earth left to discover
Is that which was the beginning;
At the source of the longest river
The voice of the hidden waterfall
And the children in the apple-tree
Not known, because not looked for
But heard, half-heard, in the stillness
Between two waves of the sea...
And all shall be well and
All manner of thing shall be well
When the tongues of flame are in-folded
Unto the crowned knot of fire
And the fire and the rose are one.

(T.S.Eliot, 1886-1965, written 1942, republ. in Four Quartets, 1944)

AUTUMN 1964

(FOR KAREN)

Red apples hang like globes of light
  Against this pale November haze,
And now, although the mist is white,
  In half-an-hour a day of days
Will climb into its golden height
  And Sunday bells will ring its praise.

The sparkling flint, the darkling yew
  The red brick, less intensely red
Than hawthorn berries bright with dew
  Or leaves of creeper still unshed,
The watery sky washed clean and new
  Are all rejoicing with the dead.

The yellowing elm shows yet some green,
  The mellowing bells exultant sound:
Never have light and colour been
  So prodigally thrown around;
And in the bells the promise tells
  Of greater light where Love is found.

(John Betjeman 1906-1984)

---

from ELEVEN ADDRESSES TO THE LORD

1

Master of beauty, craftsman of the snowflake,
inimitable contriver,
endower of Earth so gorgeous & different from the boring Moon,
thank you for such as it is my gift.

I have made up a morning prayer to you
containing with precision everything that most matters.
`According to thy will` the thing begins.
It took me off & on two days. It does not aim at eloquence.

You have come to my rescue again & again
in my impassable, sometimes despairing years.
You have allowed my brilliant friends to destroy themselves
and I am still here, severely damaged, but functioning.

Unknowable, as I am unknown to my guinea pigs:
how can I `love` you?
I only as far as gratitude & awe
confidently and absolutely go.

I have no idea whether we live again.
It doesn't seem likely
from either the scientific or the philosophical point of view
but certainly all things are possible to you,

and I believe as fixedly in the Resurrection - appearances to
Peter and to Paul
as I believe I sit in this blue chair.
Only that may have been a special case
to establish their initiatory faith.

Whatever your end may be, accept my amazement.
May I stand until death forever at attention
for any your least instruction or enlightenment.
I even feel sure you will assist me again, Master of insight & beauty.

(John Berryman, 1914-1972, publ. 1971)

EDEN ROCK

They are waiting for me somewhere beyond Eden Rock:
My father, twenty-five, in the same suit
Of Genuine Irish Tweed, his terrier Jack
Still two years old and trembling at his feet.

My mother, twenty-three, in a sprigged dress
Drawn at the waist, ribbon in her straw hat,
Has spread the stiff white cloth over the grass.
Her hair, the colour of wheat, takes on the light.

She pours tea from a Thermos, the milk straight
From an old H.P. sauce-bottle, a screw
Of paper for a cork; slowly sets out
The same three plates, the tin cups painted blue.

The sky whitens as if lit by three suns.
My mother shades her eyes and looks my way
Over the drifted stream. My father spins
A stone along the water. Leisurely

They beckon to me from the other bank.
I hear them call, `See where the stream-path is!
Crossing is not as hard as you might think. `

I had not thought it would be like this.

(Charles Causley, 1917-2003, publ. in A Field of Vision, 1988)

`Sleeping At Last`

Fear no more the heat o' the sun,
Nor the furious winter's rages; …

(Shakespeare, `Dirge` from Cymbeline)

"Say that Frau Goethe is unable to come, she is busy dying".

(Goethe's mother's last words)

… "I am old and have seen
Many things that have been,
Both grief and peace,
And wane and increase.
No tale I tell
Of ill or well,
But this I say,
Night treadeth on day,
And for worst and best
Right good is rest."

(William Morris, 1834-1896, `Lines for a Bed at Kelmscott Manor`)

LAST POEM

They have put my bed beside the unpainted screen:
They have shifted my stove in front of the blue curtain.
I listen to my grandchildren reading me a book;
I watch the servants, heating up my soup.
With rapid pencil I answer the poems of friends.
I feel in my pocket and pull out medicine-money,
When this superintendence of trifling affairs is done
I lie back on my pillows and sleep with my face to the South.

(Po Chu-I 772-846 AD, transl. by Arthur Waley, publ. in Georgina Battiscombe, Winter Song)

FEAR NO MORE

Fear no more the heat o' the sun
Nor the furious winter's rages;
Thou thy worldly task hast done,
Home art gone, and ta'en thy wages;...

Fear no more the frown o' the great,
Thou art past the tyrant's stroke;
Care no more to clothe and eat;
To thee the reed is as the oak:
The sceptre, learning, physic, must
All follow this and come to dust.

Fear no more the lightning-flash,
Nor the all-dreaded thunder-stone;
Fear not slander, censure rash;
Thou hast finished joy and moan. ...

No exorciser harm thee!
Nor no witchcraft charm thee!
Ghost unlaid forbear thee!
Nothing ill come near thee! ...

(Shakespeare, 1564-1617. Dirge from Cymbeline)

SAFE WHERE I CANNOT LIE YET

Safe where I cannot lie yet,
  Safe where I hope to lie too,
Safe from the fume and the fret;
  You, and you,
Whom I never forget.

Safe from the frost and the snow,
  Safe from the storm and the sun,
Safe where the seeds wait to grow
  One by one
And to come back in blow.

(Christina Rossetti, 1830-1894, written before 1893)

SLEEPING AT LAST

Sleeping at last, the trouble and tumult over,
  Sleeping at last, the struggle and horror past,
Cold and white, out of sight of friend and of lover
  Sleeping at last.

No more a tired heart downcast or overcast,
No more pangs that wring or shifting fears that hover,
  Sleeping at last in a dreamless sleep locked fast.

Fast asleep. Singing birds in their leafy cover
  Cannot wake her, nor shake her the gusty blast.
Under the purple thyme and the purple clover
  Sleeping at last.

(Christina Rossetti's last poem)

MARGARITAE SORORI

A late lark twitters from the quiet skies,
And from the west,
Where the sun, his day's work ended,
Lingers as in content,
There falls on the old gray city
An influence luminous and serene,
A shining peace.

The smoke ascends
In a rosy-and-golden haze. The spires
Shine and are changed. In the valley
Shadows rise. The lark sings on. The sun,
Closing his benediction,
Sinks, and the darkening air
Thrills with a sense of the triumphing night –
Night with her gift of stars
And her great gift of sleep.

So be my passing!
My task accomplished and the long day done,
My wages taken, and in my heart
Some late lark singing,
Let me be gathered to the quiet west,
The sundown splendid and serene,
Death.

(W.E.Henley, 1849-1903)

COME, DEATH

Why dost thou dally, Death, and tarry on the way?
When I have summoned thee with prayers and tears, why dost thou stay?
Come, Death, and carry now my soul away.

Wilt thou not come for calling, must I show
Force to constrain thy quick attention to my woe?
I have a hand upon thy Coat, and will
Not let thee go.

How foolish are the words of the old monks,
In Life remember Death.
Who would forget
Thou closer hangst on every finished breath?

How vain the work of Christianity
To teach humanity
Courage in its mortality.
Who would not rather die

And quiet lie
Beneath the sod
With or without a god?

Foolish illusion, what has Life to give?
Why should man more fear Death than fear to live?

(Stevie Smith 1902-1971)

MY HEART GOES OUT

My heart goes out to my Creator in love
Who gave me Death, as end and remedy.
All living creatures come to quiet Death
For him to eat up their activity
And give them nothing, which is what they want although
When they are living they do not think so.

(Stevie Smith 1902-1971)

SONNET LXXXIX

(from 100 Love Sonnets)

When I die, I want your hands on my eyes:
I want the light and wheat of your beloved hands
to pass their freshness over me once more:
I want to feel the softness that changed my destiny.

I want you to live while I wait for you, asleep.
I want your ears still to hear the wind, I want you
to sniff the sea's aroma that we loved together,
to continue to walk on the sand we walk on.

I want what I love to continue to live,
and you whom I love and sang above everything else
to continue to nourish, full-flowered:

so that you can reach everything my love directs you to,
so that my shadow can travel along in your hair,
so that everything can learn the reason for my song.

(Pablo Neruda, 1904-1973, transl. by Stephen Tapscott)

SKALD'S DEATH

I have known all the storms that roll.
I have been a singer after the fashion
Of my people – a poet of passion.
All that is past.
Quiet has come into my soul.
Life's tempest is done.
I lie at last
A bird cliff under the midnight sun.

(Hugh MacDiarmid, 1892-1978)

........When I walk out there will be nothing missing
That I can see;
The pond will be there with its fish,
The rosemary

Spreading itself over the garden
As if still aided by my hand;
The mulberry-tree I planted, and the cherry,
The old apple-trees and

The plums stretching up against the wall
Over which the church-tower still looks;
Starlings and swallows, the swans flying over,
And always the rooks.

And that distance into which I shall have vanished
Will still be there;
It was always dear to me, is now
In the thickening air.

No distance was ever like this one
The flat land with its willows, and the great sky
With the river reflecting its uncertainty
But no more I.

(C. H. Sisson,1914-2003, *from* 'Burrington Combe' in
Collected Poems 1943-1983, Carcanet Press, 1984)

HEAVEN TO BE

When I'd picture my death, I would be lying on my back,
and my spirit would rise to my belly-skin and out
like a sheet of wax paper the shape of a girl, furl
over from supine to prone and like the djinn's
carpet begin to fly, low
over our planet – heaven to be
unhurtable, and able to see without
cease or stint or stopperage,
to lie on the air, and look, and look,
not so different from my life, I would be
sheer with an almost not sore loneness,
looking at the earth as if seeing the earth
were my version of having a soul. But then
I could see my beloved, sort of standing
beside a kind of door in the sky –
not the door to the constellations,
to the pentangles, and borealis,
but a tiny flap at the bottom of the door in the
sky, like a little cat-door in the door,
through which is nothing. And he is saying to me that he must
go now, it is time. And he does not
ask me to go with him, but I feel
he would like me to with him. And I do not think
it is a living nothing, where nonbeings
can make a kind of unearthly love, I think
it's the nothing kind of nothing, I think
we go through the door and vanish together.
What depth of joy to take his arm,
pressing it against my breast
as lovers do in a formal walk,
and take that step.

(Sharon Olds, 1942 - *from* The Unswept Room, 2002)

`Epitaph for Everyman`

My heart was more disgraceful, more alone,
And more courageous than the world has known.

O passer-by, my heart was like your own.

(Frances Cornford, 1886-1966 *from* On a Calm Shore, 1960 republ.
in Frances Cornford, Selected Poems, Enitharmon Press, 1996)

Byrhtwold, the old companion, shook his ash spear and exhorted the warriors:

"Thought shall be keener, heart stronger, courage greater
as our strength grows less."

(Anon. The Battle of Maldon, 991 AD)

["Hize sceal þe heardra, Heorte þe cenre, Mod sceal
þe mare, þe ure Maezen lytlað".]

Some Interesting anthologies for further reading:

Winter Song an anthology of poems on ageing ed. Georgina Battiscombe, Constable, 1992.

The Art of Growing Older - Writers on Living and Ageing, ed. Wayne Booth, Poseidon Press, 1992

Singing in Tune with Time, Stories and Poems about Ageing, ed. Eliz. Cairns, Virago, 1993.

Poem for the Day, ed. Nicholas Albery, Chatto and Windus, 2001.

Poem for the Day 2. Chatto and Windus, 2005.

Staying Alive, ed. Neil Astley, Bloodaxe Books, 2002.

Do Not Go Gentle, Poems for Funerals, ed. Neil Astley, Bloodaxe Books, 2003.

Being Alive, ed. Neil Astley, Bloodaxe Books, 2004.

Friendship Poems ed. Peter Washington, Everyman, 1995.

Bloodaxe Book of Contemporary Women Poets, ed. Jeni Couzyn, Bloodaxe Books, 1985.

Lifelines – an anthology of poems chosen by famous people, Penguin Books, 1993.

Lifelines 2, Town House , Dublin, 1994.

Mother to Daughter, Daughter to Mother, ed. Tillie Olsen, Virago, 1985.

101 Poems to keep you Sane: emergency rations for the seriously stressed, ed. Daisy Goodwin, Harper Collins, 2001.

Japanese Death Poems: by Zen Monks and Haiku Poets on the Verge of Dying ed. Y. Hoffmann, Tuttle Publishing, Boston, Tokyo 1986.

ACKNOWLEDGMENTS

This book has been produced with the financial support of the Hedgcock Bequest administered by Brighton and Hove City Council and co-funded by the National Lottery through Awards for All. Thank you.

Every effort has been made to trace and contact copyright holders of the material published in this book. The editors apologise if any material has been included without permission or without the appropriate acknowledgement and would be glad to be told of anyone who should have been consulted.

The editors acknowledge permission to reprint copyright material as follows; we are especially grateful to all those poets and poets' representatives who most generously waived their permission fee in the cause of Age Concern:

Fleur Adcock for `Cattle in Mist`, `Things` and `Festschrift` from Poems 1960-2000 (Bloodaxe 2000); *Akwe Amosu* and the editor of Carapace, Cape Town, South Africa for `Postcard to Wolvercote Cemetery`; *Connie Bensley* for `Mr and Mrs R and the Christmas Card List` from Choosing to be a Swan (Bloodaxe 1994); Kate Donohue for *John Berryman*'s `Eleven Addresses to the Lord, 1`, and `He Resigns`; Candida Lycett Green for *John Betjeman*'s `Old Friends`, `The Last Laugh` and `Autumn 1964`; Mrs. Diana Boston for *Lucy Boston*'s `Farewell to a Trappist`; David Winter and Son Ltd. Dundee, for *Mary Brooksbank*'s poems and photograph from Sidlaw Breezes (1867); David Higham Associates for *Charles Causley*'s `Eden Rock`; the Trustees of the Mrs. F.C. Cornford Will Trust for *Frances Cornford*'s `Epitaph for Everyman`; *Mary Cowan* for `Sonnet - Consolation`; Frances Edmond for *Lauris Edmond's* `Anniversary` from Selected Poems 1975-1994, (Bridget Williams Books, 1994); Faber and Faber Ltd. for passages from `East Coker ` and `Little Gidding` from Collected Poems 1909-1962 by *T.S.Eliot; Ruth Fainlight* for `Handbag`; *UA Fanthorpe* for `Fanfare` (for Winifrid Fanthorpe) from `Stations Underground` in Standing To, (Peterloo, 1982); *Robert Frost*'s `Acquainted with the night` from The Poetry of Robert Frost, edited by Edward Connery Lathem, (Jonathan Cape, 1971, reprinted by permission of The Random House Group Ltd.; Carcanet Press Ltd. for *Robert Graves*' The Face in the Mirror`; Columbia University Press for *Han Yu*'s `A Pond in a Jardiniere` from The Columbian Book of Chinese Poetry from early times to the 13th century, ed. Burton Watson, 1984; *Barbara Hardy* for `The Photograph` from The Yellow Gospel, 2006; Faber and Faber Ltd. for `A Call` from The Spirit Level (1996) by *Seamus Heaney; Rodney Hillman* for `Francis at Madron`; Bloodaxe Books Ltd. for *Miroslav Holub*'s `Sisyphus` from his Poems Before and After: New Expanded Edition (Bloodaxe Books, 1991, 2006); Enitharmon Press for *Frances Horovitz' s* `In Painswick Churchyard`; David Higham Associates for *Elizabeth Jennings*'s `Friendship` from New Collected Poems, (Carcanet 2002); *Jenny Joseph* for `A Patient Old Cripple`, part of `Life and Turgid Times of A. Citizen`, in her Selected Poems (Bloodaxe Books, 1992); *Patrick Kavanagh's* `In Memory of My Mother`, reprinted from Collected Poems, ed. Antoinette Quinn (Allen Lane, 2004) by kind permission of the Trustees of the Estate of the late Katherine B. Kavanagh, through the Jonathan Williams Literary Agency; *Judith Kazantzis* for `When in the World` from Just after Midnight, (Enitharmon, 2004); *Lotte Kramer* for `On Shutting the Door,` `Barricades` and `Stocktaking` from Selected and New Poems 1980-1997, (Rockingham Press 1997); Faber and Faber Ltd. for *Philip Larkin*'s `Reference Back` and `Aubade` from his Collected Poems, 1990; *Laurence Lerner* for `Residues`; Faber and Faber Ltd. for `To My Friends` from Collected Poems by *Primo Levi*; Deirdre Grieve for *Hugh MacDiarmid*' s `Skald's Death` from Selected Poems, (Carcanet 1992 ); *Roger McGough*'s `Bearhugs` from Defying Gravity, (Viking-Penguin Books 1992) by permission of PFD; David Higham Associates for

Louis MacNeice's `Soapsuds`; A. M. Heath and Co. for *Edna St. Vincent Millay*'s `Time does not bring relief`` and `Dirge without Music` from Collected Poems; Carcanet Press Ltd. for *Sasha Moorsom*'s `Jewels in My Hand` from her Your Head in Mine, 1994; Carcanet Press for *Edwin Morgan*'s `The Glass` and `Coals` from his New Selected Poems, 2000 ; Carlton Books for `Portrait of the Artist as a Prematurely Old Man` from Candy is Dandy The Best of Ogden Nash by *Ogden Nash* with an Introduction by Anthony Burgess, (Andre Deutsch 1985); University of Texas Press for *Pablo Neruda*'s `Sonnet LXXXIX` from 100 Love Sonnets, transl. Stephen Tapscott, 1986; *Grace Nichols* for `Praise Song for My Mother` from The Fat Black Woman's Poems, (Virago 1984); David Higham Associates for *Norman Nicholson*'s `The Tune the Old Cow Died Of`` from his Collected Poems (Faber and Faber 1994); `Heaven to be` from The Unswept Room by *Sharon Olds*, (Jonathan Cape, 2003), reprinted by permission of the Random House Group Ltd; Faber and Faber Ltd. for `Ancient Music` from Collected Shorter Poems by *Ezra Pound;* Faber and Faber Ltd. for `Wish for a Young Wife` and `The Happy Three` from Collected Poems (1969) by *Theodore Roethke*; Russell and Volkening, Inc. for *May Sarton*'s `The Silence Now`; Bloodaxe Books for *Carole Satyamurti*'s `Intensive Care` from her Stitching in the Dark: New and Selected Poems, 2005; *David Shepherd* for `Reply to Dylan Thomas`; Carcanet Press for *C. H. Sisson*'s lines from `Burrington Combe`, Collected Poems 1943-1983 (1984); *Stevie Smith*'s `Come Death` by permission of the Estate of James MacGibbon; David Higham Associates for *Dylan Thomas'* `Do not go gentle into that good night` from Dylan Thomas, Collected Poems, Dent; for *R. S. Thomas*'s `I look out over the timeless sea`, `Portrait`, `No Time` and `The pretences are done with` from R.S.Thomas, Collected Later Poems 1988-2000, (Bloodaxe, 2004); *Derek Walcott* for `Sea Canes`; John and Anne Robinson for the Arthur Waley Estate for *Arthur Waley*'s translations from the Chinese; *Diana Ward-Davis* for `Long-legged Allure`; *Sarah Wardle* for `Full Moon with my Grandmother` from Fields Away, (Bloodaxe, 2003); A.P.Watt Ltd on behalf of Michael B Yeats for *W.B.Yeats*' `The Secrets of the Old` and `Beautiful Lofty Things`.

Other acknowledgements have been made at the foot of the relevant poems as requested by the copyright holders.

Special thanks are due to Vicky East, at the University of Sussex Printing and Reprographics Unit, for her skill, patience and hard work in taking an error-strewn floppy disk and converting it into this book.

We are also most grateful to Fiona Adamczewski, Val Enderby, Dorothy Engmann, Rodney Hillman, and Joanna Reid for their responsiveness and suggestions.

Derek Oldfield and Roy Shaw (see back cover) were their usual benign selves.

Verses on death of Dr. Swift
1731

Index of writers